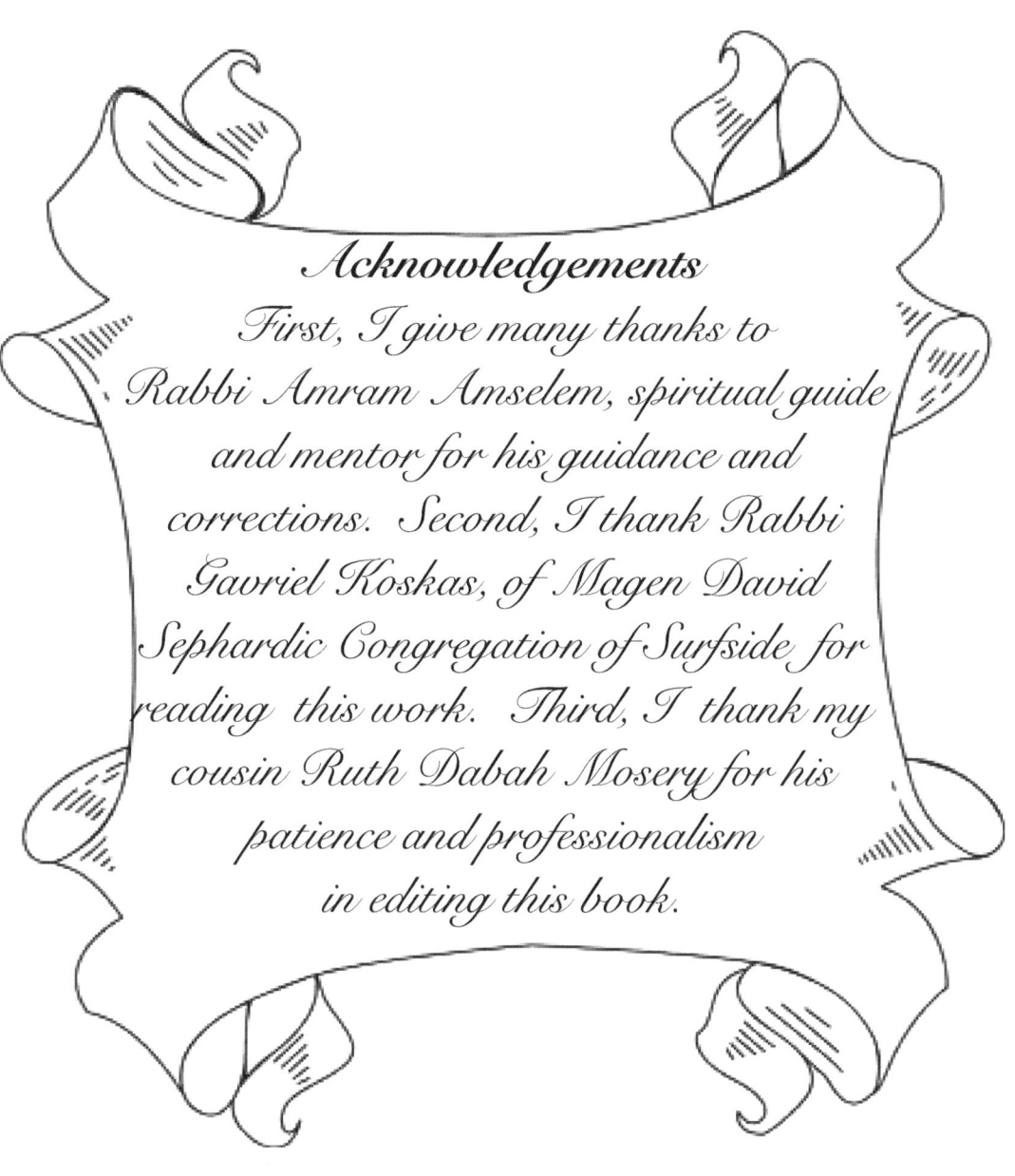

Acknowledgements

First, I give many thanks to Rabbi Amram Amselem, spiritual guide and mentor for his guidance and corrections. Second, I thank Rabbi Gavriel Koskas, of Magen David Sephardic Congregation of Surfside for reading this work. Third, I thank my cousin Ruth Dabah Mosery for his patience and professionalism in editing this book.

In Memory of my dear
Mother Sara Bassan Bat Malca Z"L
who was always available to her
family, community and Israel.

In Memory of my Grandmother
Malca Cohen Bat Sara Z"L
who always read her Hebrew Bible
she brought from Israel.

In Memory of my Grandmother
Raquel Bassan Bat Simcha Z"L who
chose to live near the Shaare Zion
Synagogue with her husband in
Brooklyin, New York.

In Memory of my Grandfathers
Nessim Bassan Ben Esther Z"L &
Elias Cohen Ben Husny Z"L
who were the first spokesperson and
treasurer respectfully of the Shevet
Ahim Congregation of Panama.

LESSONS OF THE PROPHETS
by
MALCA BASSAN

SOON IN OUR DAYS

Introduction

In the year 2003, a book by the name of **For Your Own Good** was published by the author of this work. It contained a summary of all the weekly Torah portions of the Five Books of Moses read in the Shabbat day. Each portion was illustrated by a painted drawing representing the message. After the publication in 2003, the author thought of a second part that will illustrate the portion read after the Torah portion every Shabbat. This one is known as haftarah, הפטרה, because the root of the word פטר, means "to take leave." In other words, after the reading of the main Torah portion we "take leave" or "we conclude the service by reading the haftarah.

In the time of the Emperor Antiochus in the period of the Chashmonaim, according to the Levush (see glossary), the reading of the Torah portion during Shabbat was prohibited. As a result, the Sages of the time substituted them with portions of the prophets in the Bible that are related to each one of the Torah portions. Even after the prohibition was canceled, the Rabbis decided to continue with the readings of the prophets.

In general, the haftarah of Shabbat contains at least 21 verses that corresponds to the 21 verses or more of the Torah portion. Since 7 men are called up to the Torah portion on Shabbat, each one should read or listen at least 3 verses. Both the Torah portion and the haftarah need to be more or equal in the amount of verses. During holidays, each haftarah contains at least 15 verses because 5 men are called up to the Torah portion. Each one should read or listen 3 verses. It is not obligatory to read the haftarah from a handwritten parchment, however, some communities in Jerusalem use a Torah scroll instead of a book to read the haftarah.

The name of this work, **Soon In Our Days,** teaches and illustrates the messages of the prophets to the Jewish people. This book focus in making the necessary soul corrections as divine human beings, so we can strengthen our faith for the future.

Table of Contents

Blessings of the Haftarah..9

Haftarahs from the Book of Beresheet............................14

Haftarahs from the Book of Shemot................................40

Haftarahs from the Book of Vayikra.................................61

Haftarahs from the Book of Bamidbar..............................84

Haftarahs from the Book of Devarim...............................106

Haftarahs from the Jewish Holidays and Fast Days......... 132

Brief Outline of Each Prophet... 186

Glossary..206

About the Author...209

Copyright..211

Blessings of the Haftarah

There are a total of five blessings read over the haftarah: one before the haftarah and four after.

Blessing # 1: Thanks to Hashem for granting us Prophets.

ברוך אתה ה'' אלה-ינו מלך העולם
אשר בחר בינביאים טובים
ורצה בידבריכם הנאמרים באמת.
ברוך אתה ה'' הבוחר בתורה
ובמשה עבדו ובישראל עמו
ובינביאי האמת וצדק:

Blessed are you, Hashem, our G-d. King of the Universe, Who chose worthy prophets *(with the proper qualifications: wise, physically strong, humble, rich and tall so as to command respect)* and accepted with pleasure their words that were spoken in truth. *(All their words were spoken with ruach hakodesh.)* Blessed are You, Hashem, Who has chosen the Torah, His servant Moshe, His people Yisrael, and prophets of truth and justice. the turre prophets exhort Bnai Yisrael to keep the Torah which is the epitome of truth and justice.)

After Blessings of the Haftarah

Blessing # 2: Hashem fulfills the Prophets' words.

ברוך אתה ה'' אלה-ינו מלך העולם, צור כל העולמים, צדיק בכל הדורות, הא-ל הנאמן האומר ועושה, המדבר ומקים, שכל דבריו אמת וצדק: נאמן, אתה הוא ה'' אלה-ינו, ונאמנים דבריך, ודבר אחד מדבריך אחור לא ישוב ריקם, כי א-ל מלך נאמן ורחמן אתה. ברוך אתה ה'', הא-ל הנאמן בכל דבריו:

Blessed are You, Hashem, our G-d, King of the Universe. Rock of all the worlds, a tzaddik in all generations, the faithfulwords are truth and justice. Faithful are You. Hashem our G-d, and faithful are Your words. Not one of Your words ever goes unfulfilled, for You are a faithful and merciful G-d and king. Blessed are You, Hashem Who is faithful in all His words.

Blessing # 3: Request of Redemption

רחם על ציון כי היא בית חיינו, ולעלובת נפש תושיע במהרה בימנו. ברוך אתה ה'', משמח ציון בבניה:

Have mercy on Tzion, by gathering in the exiles and rebuilding the Beit Hamikdash, for she (Tzion) is the home (source) of life. Help the downcast Jewish nation **soon in our days**. Blessed are You, Hashem Who causes Tzion to rejoice with her children.

After Blessings of the Haftarah

Blessing # 4: Request for the Restoration of the Davidic Dynasty

שמחנו, ה'' אלה-ינו, באליהו הנביא עבדך, ובמלכות בית דוד משיחך,
במהרה יבוא ויגל לבנו, על כסאו לא ישב זר,
ולא ינחלו עוד אחרים את כבודו,
כי בשם קדשך נשבעת לו, שלא יכבה נרו לעולם ועד.
ברוך אתה ה'', מגן דוד:

    Let us rejoice, our G-d, with the arrival of Your servant Eliyahu HaNavi and with the kingdom of the house of David. Your anointed. Let him (Eliyahu) soon arrive and cheer our hearts. Let no stranger sit on his (David's) throne and may others no longer inherit his glory, for You have sworn to him by Your holy Name that his light will never be extinguish. Blessed are You, Hashem, **Shield of David.**

After Blessings of the Haftarah

Blessing # 5: Thanks for the Shabbat and the Special Service of the Day.

על התורה, ועל העבודה ועל הנביאים ועל יום השבת הזה,
שנתת לנו ה'' אלה-ינו לקדושה ולמנוחה,
לכבוד ולתפארת: על הכל, ה'' אל-הינו, אנחנו מודים לך, ומברכים אותך,
יתברך שמך בפי כל תמיד לעולם ועד.   ברוך אתה ה'' מקדש השבת:

For the Torah which we read previously and for the avoda - our prayers that are in place of the service in the Beit Hamikdash - and for the Prophets - the Haftarah - and for this Shabbat which You, Hashem, our G-d, gave us for sanctity, rest, honor and glory - for all the above, we thank You and bless you. Your name shall be praised by every living being forever. Blessed are You, Hashem, Who sanctifies the Shabbat:

Book of Beresheet

Genesis

Haftarah Beresheet
Isaiah 42:5-43:10

> **Mashiach will open our eyes**

Galut comes from the Hebrew "Ga-lo," meaning "to discover." Galut is any place outside of Israel, because we should learn about G-d there too. Mashiach will open our eyes to discover G-d by way of the Torah that comes from Israel.

G-d will sing His last song and will reveal the secret of the mitzvoth and good deeds. He will show us the way to the Land of milk and honey.

Each mitzvah is a ticket to enter the World to Come. If we focus in a specific mitzvah and observe it responsibly, we will acquire this ticket for our own good.

Haftarah Noach
*I*saiah 54:1-10

The words of Torah are like the water, milk and wine. In the same way that these are kept fresh in containers made of plastic, cardboard and glass, the words of Torah are freshly preserved in humble bodies.

> ***The mabul or flood was named "the waters of Noah***

The mabul or flood was named "the waters of Noah," so that the people would return to G-d like the waves come back to the sea.

Noah built the ark to protect himself from the flood. Likewise, G-d wants us to build our own apartment with special bricks of Charity and Torah.

Haftarah Lech Lecha
Isaiah 40:27-41:16

Abraham was known as the light of the Orient because his faith in G-d brightened up the nations.

G-d said to Abraham to leave his land in the Orient, and walk to the land that He will show him. It wasn't easy to make a decision so quickly.

> **his faith in G-d brightened up the nations**

Both Abraham, son of Terach, and Shem, son of Noah, showed their faith in G-d like two islands in an ocean of idols. Shem was named the carpenter because he helped his father Noah to build the ark.

Abraham was named the "man of the hammer," because with nails of Tefillah (prayer) and mitzvoth, he perfected his faith in G-d.

Both Abraham and Noach showed their faith in G-d like two islands in an ocean of idols.

Haftarah Vayera
Kings II 4:1-37

The Jewish king Ahab got married to queen Hezabel. She criticized the Jewish prophets because she did not like them. King Ahab worked with Obadiah to protect the prophets from the evil queen. Obadiah defended them, and hid them in caves.

> **Obadiah defended them, and hid them in caves**

Since Obadiah lost his fortune, he could not save any more prophets from the evil queen. Then, Obadiah had an idea, and he asked Yehoram for a loan. He was the son of king Ahab who lent him the money but with interest.

Obadiah became ill, and owed a great deal of money to Yehoram as a result of the interest. The wife of Obadiah asked him, "What would you do?" Obadiah answered her, "G-d will provide."

Elisha asked her to bring empty vases. He took the vase with the oil and was able to fill up all the others with this liquid. The first vase blessed her, and her family for many years. The words of Obadiah turned out to be true because G-d provided her and her family with what they needed.

Poor Obadiah passed on, and Yehoram stole his two sons as payment. Obadiah's respected wife invited Elisha to eat at her house. "What do you have of value in your home?" Elisha asked her. "I only have oil in a vase." She answered.

Haftarah Haye Sarah
Kings I 1:1-31

While Saul was the king of Israel, the prophet Samuel appointed David as the next king. As a result, Saul was envious and immediately started to run after David.

Saul and David entered the same cave. David cut a piece of Saul´s coat, without him noticing it. In spite of Saul´s envy towards him, David honored him and respected him. He prepared a banquet on top of a rock named "Zochelet."

> *In spite of Saul´s envy, David honored him*

Why did David make a banquet on top of this rock? "Zochelet" which comes from the root "Zachal," that means to crawl. Anyone who tries to go after David's throne, would crawl like a serpent.

King Shlomo said, "Two are better than one."   King David and Batsheva were the parents who brought him into this world. Prophet Nathan blessed David and Batsheva.

The blessing guaranteed that Adoniyahu, Shlomo's brother, would not be the next king.

Adoniyahu declared himself king in a great banquet.
He invited all of his siblings except Shlomo. In the end, the blessing of prophet Nathan was remembered, and Shlomo became the king of Israel.

Haftarah Toldot
Malachi 1:1 – 2:7

"G-d loves Yaakov who represents peace, and dislikes Esav who represents lie," said Malachi, the last of the Jewish prophets.

> "To honor the Name of G-d, one has to give Him from the best that we own."

Malachi rebuked the Kohanim because they did not do their work with good will. He used to tell them, "A child is obligated to honor his father, as the Jews are obligated to honor G-d." We should learn from Esav, that even though he was a liar, he served his father Isaac LIKE KING.

Malachi rebuked the Jews for their own good. Sometimes they did not bring the best to the Temple of Jerusalem. He said to them, "To honor the Name of G-d, one has to give Him from the best that we own."

What is Malachi suggesting? His words teach us that in every generation, each Jew must behave like a Kohen. A Kohen is an emissary that G-d sends so that we will serve Him wholeheartedly. For this reason, each Jew should teach Torah with love and good will.

Haftarah Vayetze
Hoshea 11:7 – 14:10

Reuben, the firstborn of Yaakov, was connecting to G-d, whereas his brothers were busy with the sale of their little brother Josef.

Reuben was the first person who returned to G-d with heart and soul. He was the first who made Teshuva.

> **Reuben was the first person who returned to G-d**

G-d rewarded Reuben by giving him a descendant who reawakened the teshuva process. Hoshea the prophet was the one.

When the twelve tribes of Israel were divided into two kingdoms, Hoshea rebuked the kingdom of the Ten Tribes, to make them believe in ONLY ONE G-D.

How did he accomplish it? Hoshea the prophet reminded them of our father's deeds. Even though Yaakov lived surrounded by the idols of his father in law Laban, he observed the 613 mitzvoth of the Torah. As a result, G-d rewarded Yaakov with good fortune.

Hoshea the prophet always said, "Although the Jews are far from G-d, all of them will return like a dove to the Land of Israel."

Haftarah Vayishlach
Obadiah 1:1-21

> **Esav's children were known as Edomites.**

Obadiah was a righteous Edomite who lived among the evil kings Ahab and Hezabel.
Similarly, Esav lived in the midst of a generous family, formed by his parents Isaac, Rebecca and his brother Yaakov.
Esav's children were known as Edomites. They lived south of the Land of Israel.

Yaakov thought that his son Josef, the righteous, was the only one who could confront Esav.

Josef lived in Egypt and believed in G-d. Esav lived in Israel with his father, and his lies moved him away from G-d.
Esav always looked for power, Yaakov walked with the light of Torah. As long as we unite with Yaakov and isolate from Esav, the sooner Edom would fall.

Haftarah Vayeshev
Amos 2:6 – 3:8

The Midrash says that after the brothers of Josef sold him, they bought shoes with the payment. Another Midrash says that only the upper class wore shoes in those times.

This teaches us that the brothers of Josef regarded themselves free whereas his brother was sold as a slave.

Haftarah Miketz
Kings I - 3:15 – 4:1

After his twelfth birthday, Shlomo was appointed king of Israel.
As a result of a dream he had, he was granted a wish. King Shlomo asked for intelligence and wisdom.

King Shlomo took advantage of his wisdom to learn Torah, and thus, he organized a great feast when he finished studying it.
King Shlomo invited all of the judges of the Sanhedrin, and taught them to make a celebration when they finish learning a portion of the Torah. This ceremony is known in Hebrew as a "Siyum." When we celebrate a "Siyum," we honor even more the Torah with joy and thanks.

The intelligence of King Shlomo was demonstrated with the trial of the baby. Two mothers came to him, fighting among themselves for a baby. Each one said that the baby belonged to her. In that moment, King Shlomo commanded to cut the baby in two. "In this way," he said, "both women could share the baby." What happened at the end? One of the mothers screamed, "Don't cut him!" King Shlomo decided that this was the real mother because she showed compassion instantly.

Haftarah Vayigash
Ezekiel 37:15 – 28

When King Shlomo passed on, the Land of Israel was divided into two kingdoms. The smaller one was the kingdom of Yehuda and Benjamin, while the bigger one was the kingdom of the Ten Tribes.

G-d let the Land of Israel be separated into two kingdoms because King Shlomo was too pleasing with his wives, something that should not have happened.

> **Thank G-d, today there are not two kingdoms, but instead, there are many communities**

Prophet Ezekiel took two pieces of wood, one for each kingdom. He joined both of them, and in this way, showed how both kingdoms would be united in the future. Thank G-d, today there are not two kingdoms, but instead, there are many communities. Each one functions according to the Torah, the Halacha and their own customs. King Shlomo teaches us that we have to be united.
WE HAVE TO LEARN THE GOOD OF EACH COMMUNITY, AND RESPECT THEIR THE DIFFERENCES.

Haftarah Vayehi
Kings I 2:1 – 12

Yaakov our father never died. He united all of his children and blessed them, before leaving to the World to Come. All his children were righteous.

> **He united all of his children**

King David lives forever. He got together with his son Shlomo before departing to the World to Come, and said to him, "You have the honesty to be the next king of Israel."

Book of Shemot Exodus

Haftarah Shemot
Isaiah 27:6 – 28:13, 29:22 – 23 (Ashkenazi custom)
Yirmiyahu 1:1 – 2:3 (Sephardi custom)

The Jews from the kingdom of Israel ate and drank without mentioning words of Torah. Isaiah, the prophet, showed them the way of G-d in an easy manner, and still, did not listened.

The prophet said over and over, that if they did not observe the Torah, their enemies would manipulate them.

From that point on, king Chizkiyahu removed the idols from the Land of Israel, teaching them the way of the Torah.

Thanks to king Chizkiyahu, the Jews returned to G-d. From him came Yirmiyahu, the Kohen, who refused to be prophet for two reasons. First, because he could not pronounce the words clearly, and second, because he did not want to be
the agent of bad news about the future of Israel.

Once, prophet Yirmiyahu saw an almond tree. This plant flourishes faster than any other. In the same way, the Temple of Jerusalem would flourish.

Haftarah Vaera
Ezekiel 28:25 – 29:21

The Egyptian kings were called Pharaohs. The Pharaoh who had a relationship with the Nile river. He said, "This is my river that gives me everything without the help of G-d." **As a result, the Pharaoh was considered the great crocodile of the Nile river.**

Then, G-d sent king Nebuchadnezzar of Babylon to defeat the Egyptian Pharaoh. Since Nebuchadnezzar fought against the nations of Tyre and Sidon, G-d placed him in a higher level than Pharaoh. At this moment, Egypt ceased to be the Great Nation.

Haftarah Bo
Yirmiyahu 46:13 – 28

The Egyptian soldiers were as many as the trees of Egypt. If the soldiers had not repented, the Babylonians would have chopped down all their trees.

The name "Egypt" is "Mitzrayim" in Hebrew. It comes from the root "tzara," that means suffering and narrowness. Just as Egypt enslaved Israel with hard and forced labor, G-d will pay Egypt with the same suffering.

After the Egyptian exile, the Jews lived four more exiles: the Babylonian, the Persian, the Greek and the Edomite. G-d promised Israel that after all these four exiles, she would go back to the Promise Land. Today, we are living in the Edomite exile that is the fourth and last one.

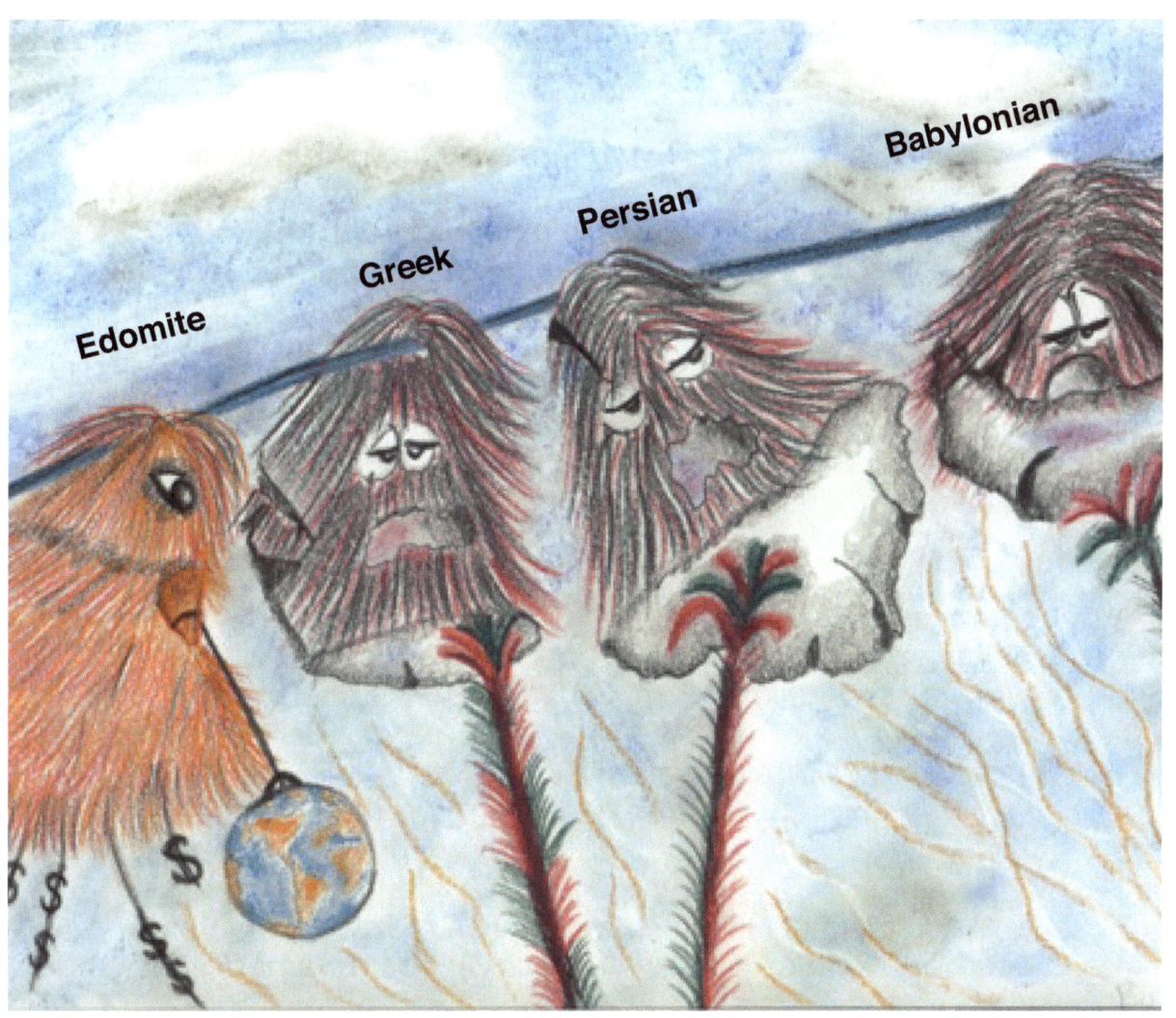

Haftarah Beshalach
Judges 4:4 – 5:31

G-d sent judges to the Jews when they behaved righteously in front of Him. Deborah, who was born from the tribe of Naphtali, used to prepare the wicks of the Menorah in the Temple. She had the merit to be judge of Israel, and to inspire her husband Barack, and the Jews of her time, to follow the way of the Torah.

Deborah educated Israel throughout her prophecies. In one occasion, she sent a messenger to Barack to inform him that he would fight against general Sisrah from the Yabin army. Barack wanted Deborah to accompany him, and to support
him in the mission.

Deborah answered Barack, "A woman would kill general Sisrah." Barack thought the woman would be Deborah.
The war was a miracle of G-d. General Sisrah escaped from the clutches of Barack, and ran until he arrived at the house of Hever the kenite from the family of Yitro. He was married to a woman named Yael.
Then, Sisrah entered Yael's tent and she looked after him. During this time Sisrah repented, but did not last for long.

Since Yael knew that Sisrah was evil, she extracted a nail from the tent and used it to injure him. When Barack finally came to her tent, she gave him a lifeless Sisrah.

Haftarah Yitro
Isaiah 6:1-7:6, 9:5-6

In G-d's presence, the Jews are bigger than the angels. When the Kedusha is recited in the Amida prayer, they have the gift to bless and elevate souls.

"Kadosh, Kadosh, Kadosh, Holy, Holy, Holy," the Jews recite in the Kedusha. It means that G-d IS HOLY in the Divine World, in the modern world, and in the World to Come.

King Achaz closed all the yeshivot of the kingdom of Yehuda. He did not want the Jews to learn Torah. Prophet Isaiah and his son tried to show Achaz the way of Teshuvah or repentance. The king repented for a short while and later, went back to his wicked customs. Because of his efforts to return to G-d, He granted Achaz the World to Come.

King Achaz had a son whose name was Chizkiyahu. He was an excellent advisor who allowed the Jews to study Torah. G-d would have liked Chizkiyahu to be the Mashiach but instead, his eight names agreed with the eight missions of the Future King.

Haftarah Mishpatim
Yirmiyahu 34:8-22, 33:25-26

The Jews lived in poverty during the time of prophet Yirmiyahu. The poor sold themselves to the rich to preserve their lives.

The poor became servants of the rich for 6 years, but sometimes held them even more.

G-d did not like that the rich Jews would abuse their poor brothers. As a result, He exiled them from the Promise Land.

Haftarah Truma
Kings I 5:26, 6:13

King Shlomo finished the Temple in seven years. He worked hard for its construction. King Shlomo had to speak with Hiram king of Tyre, so that he would donate the wood for the Temple. What was so special about Tyre? Abundance of Cedar trees.

Among other things, king Shlomo did not allow the use of iron tools in the construction of the Temple. What was wrong about these tools? Iron is a kind of material used in the production of weapons for war.

This is the reason why king Shlomo used the SHAMIR to cut the wood, instead of the iron tools.

The SHAMIR was a cutting worm that was not easily found. King Shlomo checked with the "sheidim" (demons) and these answered him, "There is a bird named
Bar-Hen that helps the SHAMIR cut the wood." This bird knew where the SHAMIR was. **King Shlomo found the bird on time and next to it, the SHAMIR, that cut the wood of the Temple.**

Haftarah Tetzave
Ezekiel 43: 10-27

If the Jews strengthen their faith in the eternal Temple, they would be rewarded
with participating in its construction. Thanks to this, the Jews must learn about the design of the Holy Temple, in the same way as prophet Ezekiel taught.

The MIZBEACH is the elevation for offerings of the Temple. The word MIZBEACH has four letters in the Hebrew language. The MEM is the first letter of the word MECHILLA, forgiveness. The ZAYIN is the second letter of the word ZECHUT, merit. The BEITH is the third letter of the word BERACHA, blessing. The CHET is the fourth letter of the word CHAYIM, life. The MIZBEACH unites the Jews by way of forgiveness, merit, blessing and life.

The peak of the MIZBEACH is known with the name of ARIEL. ARIEL is referred to as one of the five miracles that happened
with the fire of the MIZBEACH. The fire formed the shape of a lion, symbol of strength. That is that the Divine Strength was manifested in the MIZBEACH.

Haftarah Ki Tissa
Kings I 18: 1-39

There was a long drought in the Land of Israel during the Kingdom of Achab. It lasted for three years and a half. G-d prohibitted the Jews to worship idols.

The only one who could end both the drought and the camine was prophet Eliyahu, to whom Achab sent emissaries.

When Eliyahu arrived at king Achab's place, he noticed that the Jews resisted in returning to G-d and continued with their old idolater customs.

The prophet let the Jews kneel down before the idols, whereas he prayed for their return to G-d.

Haftarah Vayakhel – Pekude

Kings I 7: 13-26 (Vayakhel Sephardic custom)
Kings I 7: 40-50 (Vayakhel Ashkenazi custom)
Kings I 7: 51 - 8:21 (Pekude)

Hiram the king of Tyre helped king Shlomo build the Temple. Hiram designed the objects and three columna with copper. Two columns represents Torah study and prayer while the third column represented the good deeds that the Jews should carry on. The Temple walls were decorated with carved trees. Everytime that the Holy Ark was walked around these trees, they became real. The Temple was a source of blessing.

At the end of the construction of the Temple, king Shlomo prayed that the doors would open. When he pronounced the name of his father David, his prayer was accepted. Since then, king Shlomo knew that the sin
of his father was forgiven.

Book of Vayikra Leviticus

Haftarah Vaikra
Isaiah 43:21 – 44:23

G-d is glad when the Jews gather in the Temple to sing and praise Him.

G-d calls the people of Israel with three names, according to how much faith they have in Him. When the Jews are in the lowest level of faith, He calls them "Yaakov." When the Jews are in a high level, He calls them "Israel." When the Jews are in the highest level, He calls them "Yeshurun."

When the Jews worshiped idols, they were in the lowest level of faith. Why did the Jews worship idols? Just to satisfy their tastes. The truth slipped away because the Jews did not remember they are G-d's servants. Therefore, they must follow the Truth to get it back.

When the Jews are in the **highest level**, He calls them

When the Jews are in a high level, He calls them "**Israel**."

When the Jews are in the lowest level of faith, He calls them "**Yaakov**."

Haftarah Tzav
Yirmiyahu 7:21 - 8:3, 9:22-23

G-d liberated the Jews from Egypt so that they will obey His Laws, instead of transforming them into a people who offer sacrifices.

During the time of the Prophets, the Jews worshiped idols. Because of this, G-d was not with the Jews entirely, and many events happened that hurt them. For example, the Amonites advised king
Nebuchadnezzar to breach Jerusalem on the tenth of Tevet. This was the first step towards the destruction of Jerusalem.

First, when Moses finished his mission on this world, G-d gave him his reward. Second, when Shimshon passed on, his strength expired.
Third, when king Achab died, his riches finished off.

Intelligence and strength are not forever.

The goal of the Jew is to understand

Intelligence and strength are not forever.

G‑d wants of him: to recognize His

Haftarah Shemini
Samuel II 6:1 – 7:17

King David carried the Ark walking until he arrived in Jerusalem. **At this moment, he danced with the people.** How strange? Why did he do it? David did not want the Jews to look at the Ark directly because it was forbidden. Therefore, they contemplated him dancing.

King David wished to build the Temple, when the Ark was safe in Jerusalem. Why didn't G-d let him build the Temple? If king David had built it, G-d would have destroyed it.

David did not want the Jews to look at the Ark directly because it was

Haftarah Tazria
Kings II 4:42 – 5:19

> Elisha's objective was that Naaman would get rid of his vanity.

Naaman was a soldier from the kingdom of Aram, that today is Damascus. He was a very arrogant man, and that's why, G-d punished him with a skin disease. Once, Naaman captured a Jewish girl in one of the wars between Aram and Israel. The girl tried to cure Naaman's vanity, but she was not successful. Then, she advised him to visit prophet Elisha in Israel so that he´d pray to G-d and be cured.

Riding on his horse, Naaman arrived in Israel with his army and carriages. His vanity prevented him from getting off the horse. But Elisha was wiser, and did not welcome him. Elisha sent a messenger instead. He told him, "Naaman, you should immerse yourself seven times in the waters of the Jordan river."

Elisha's objective was that Naaman of Aram would get rid of his vanity by immersing in the waters of the river.

Naaman's servants convinced him, "If the prophet had told you to do something major, wouldn't you have done it?" They asked him. "Immerse yourself, and you'd come out clean." They ordered him. Finally, Naaman immersed in the Jordan river and believed in the G-d of kindness.

Naaman wanted to pay money to Elisha for having cured him, but he did not accept nothing in return. Just a miracle of G-d could have cured Naaman. We only have to thank G-d for all that we are given.

Haftarah Metzora
Kings II 7:3-20

> Gaihazi and his three sons ran to let their brothers have part of the treasure

Our sages teach that when a Jew cures a non Jew, he should receive his salary. Elisha did not want to receive his pay for having cured Naaman because he wanted to show Naaman that his cure was a miracle of G-d.

G-d used to send famines when the Jews sinned. The only one who could beg G-d to end the drought was prophet Elisha.

During the kingdom of Yehoram, there was such a strong famine, that it was difficult to get wheat. Elisha's partner Gaihazi, and his three sons crossed the Jordan river at sunrise, and found Aram's camp with no people, only food, clothing and gold. They wanted everything they found and made themselves owners of the treasure. Later, they remembered the rest of their community.

Gaihazi and his three sons ran to let their brothers have part of the treasure, so they could satisfy their hunger as well. At the end, Elisha assured them, "The famine would end in any event, even if the treasure is shared. It is part of G-d's plan".

Haftarah Acharei Mot
Amos 9:7-15 (ashquenazi)
Ezekiel 22:1-16 (Sephardi)

The prophets of the Children of Israel criticized them for worshiping idols, and for not behaving appropriately. Only a few of them sinned, however, their bad deeds were more noticeable among the majority.

The sins are more serious when they are done in a holy site, such as Jerusalem. Because of their inappropriate behaviour, this city suffered even more because it was the holiest in the kingdom of Yehuda.

Prophet Ezekiel accused the Jews for committing 24 sins: the worst of all, was stealing, because it ruins the society. King Shlomo teaches us to learn from a colony of ants. They respect foreign properties in their own natural environment.

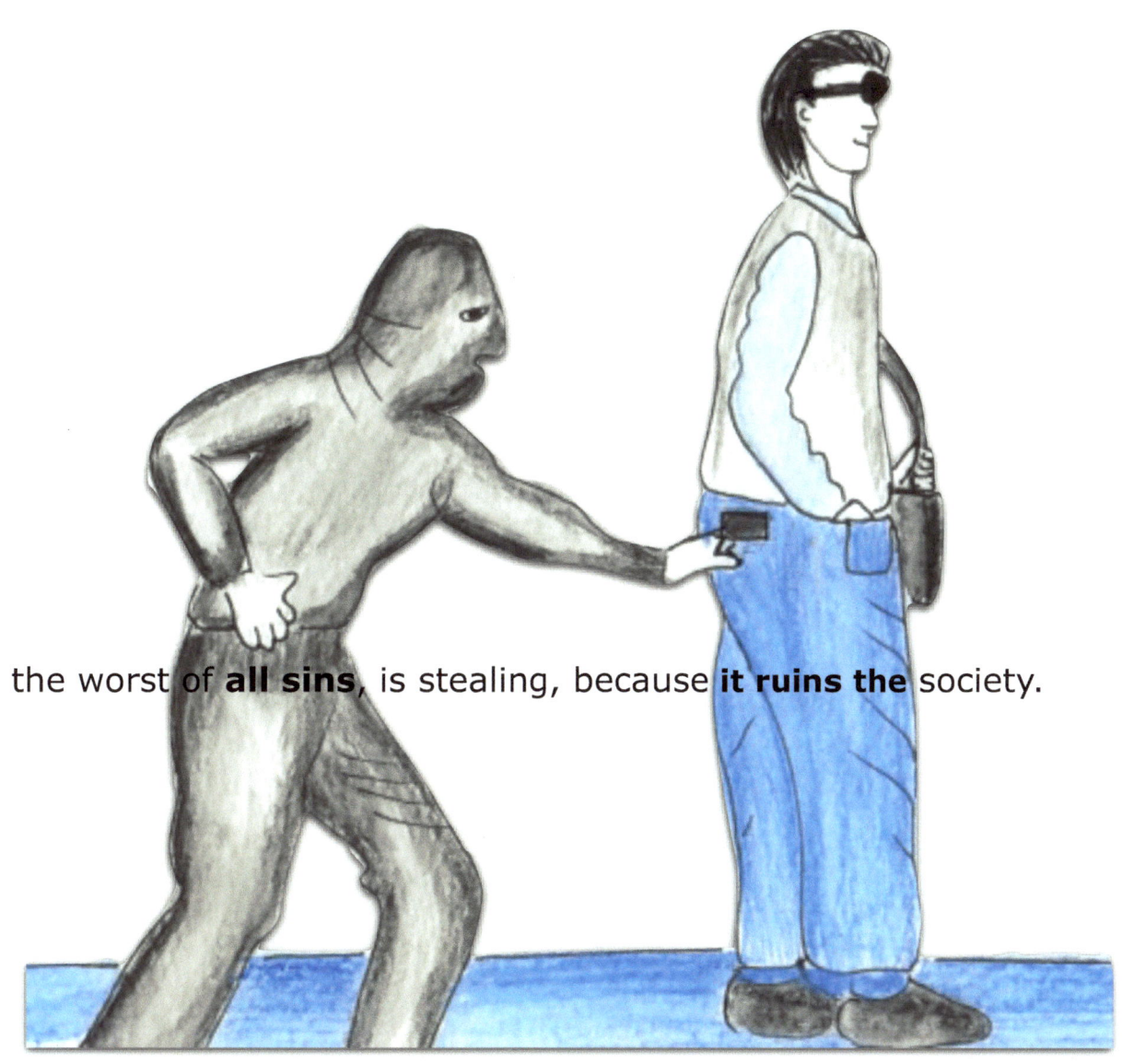

the worst of **all sins**, is stealing, because **it ruins the** society.

Haftarah Kedoshim
Ezekiel 22:1-16 (Ashkenazi)
Ezekiel 20:2-20 (Sephardi)

G-d said. "The Jews and the other nations will be sifted together like grains of flour." All the grains will be placed in the same bowl. In the same way, all the nations will share the exile under G-d's care.

The Succa of David, the Guardian of Israel, falls when its leaders do not keep the commandments of the Torah. Mashiach will be the only one who could raise the Succa of David. Only then, the unity between Israel and the Torah will be real and unique.

The Land of Israel is like the skin of a deer. As it is elastic, so is the Land that will expand according to the people's needs. As a result, it is the most desired and coveted land.

Shabbat is the most important mitzvah, because the Universe was created for her. Shabbat was the "reason to be" of Creation. This mitzvah is equivalent to all the mitzvoth together.

Haftarah Emor
Ezekiel 44-15-31

Tzadok was the first Kohen, who worked in king Shlomo's Temple. He was a righteous man. As a result, the Kohanim of Tzadok's family will be the only ones who will serve in the future Temple.

A kohen from Tzadok´s family, Matitiyahu, and his five children, fought to sanctify G-d's name. They did not let the Assyrians or Hellenists prevent them from observing their Judaism. During the Second Temple, Matitiyahu saved the Jews from their enemies.

Tzadok's family descended from the tribe of Levi. They stood out for their loyalty to G-d, as well as for teaching Torah to the Jews.

> A portion of dough needs to be separated from the bread mixture. This is called "challah," and it's for the Kohen.

The Kohen Gadol needed to be dressed all year round according to the kohen´s attire. The dress of a person represents purity. Since the Kohanim were the Torah teachers of the people, they were distinguished by how they were dressed.

A portion of dough needs to be separated from the bread mixture. This is called "challah," and it's for the Kohen. During the time of the Temple, the "challah" was given to the Kohen. Today, it is given to the needy. The "challah" brings blessing to the home.

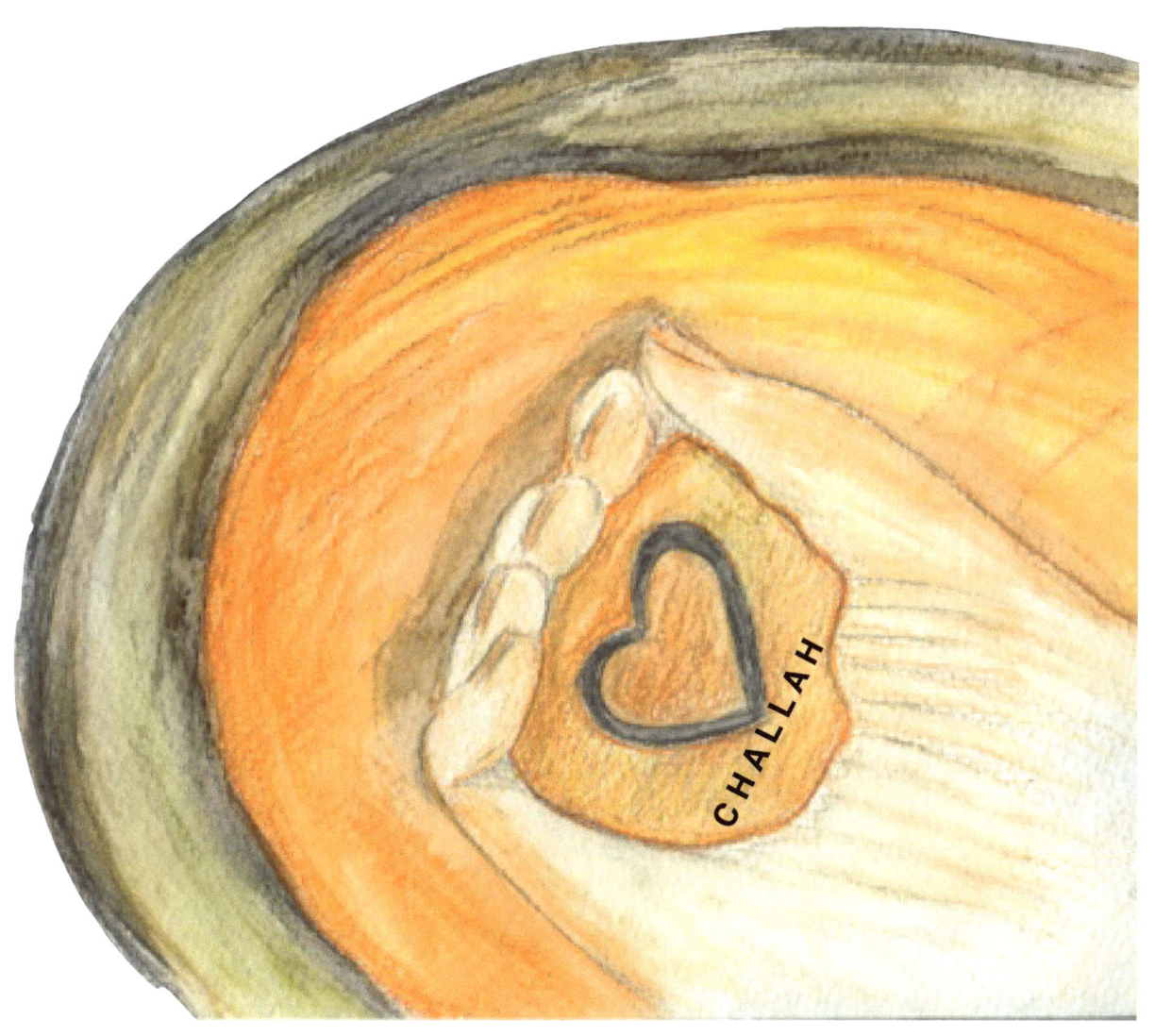

Haftarah Behar
Jeremiah 32:6-27

Prophet Yirmiyahu was a Kohen. He was born in the city of Anatot, on Benjamin's territory. Anatot was under the Chaldeans' authority. His cousin Hanamel was obligated to sell him his land because of financial problems. Selling an estate to the closest relative is a great mitzvah!

Yirmiyahu asked G-d, "Why do I have to buy my cousin's land, if the Chaldeans were going to conquer it?"
G-d answered him, "The Chaldeans will conquer Jerusalem, but the Jews will return there in the future." At this moment, the Jews will buy their lands anew.

Yirmiyahu bought Hanamel's land before the Jews left the Land of Israel because it was a Divine commandment. This contract was proof to let the people know of their future return to the Land of their ancestors.

Selling an estate to the closest relative is a great mitzvah!

Haftarah Bechukotai
Jeremiah 16:19 17:14

The Kingdom of Yehuda was "swimming" in waters of idolatry. In other words, the Jews were always thinking of idols. For this reason, they were exiled from the Promised Land.

The Jews from the kingdom of Yehuda hiked mountains in order to worship idols. Prophet Yirmiyahu called them "Harari," meaning "those who reside
in the mountains".

Besides worshiping idols, the Jews failed to observe the mitzvah of Shemita. They did not follow the agricultural rest of the Land of Israel in the seventh year.

The person who just trusts in people and not in G-d, is like a tamarind tree that grows in the hot desert lands without its fruits and leaves. Joseph trusted in G-d very much, except when he asked the Egyptian prisoners "to remember him," when they were liberated before him. G-d made Joseph stay two more years in prison for having said these three words: "**to remember him**". G-d hoped that Joseph had more trust in Him than in the prisoners.

Book of Bamidbar
Numbers

Haftarah Bamidbar
Hoshea 2:1-22

Prophet Hoshaya explains the relationship between G-d and Israel as follows: G-d is the husband, Israel is the wife, and the rest of the nations are G-d's lovers.

G-d dislikes when Israel goes after other nations. The time will come when the nations distance themselves from Israel. Then, Israel would return to G-d with all her heart, with all her soul and will all her property. Israel will name G-d, "Ishi," or "My Man," instead of, "Baali," "My Master." The relationship between G-d and Israel will be more intimate.
Israel inherited from Our father Abraham two jewels: generosity and righteousness. Israel inherited from G-d two more jewels at Sinai: kindness and compassion. When the Temple was destroyed, these two jewels were lost because Israel did not judge their fellow rightly, and for not having treated the poor with compassion. **Soon in our days,** *G-d will return these two jewels to Israel.*

G-d dislikes when the children of Israel are carried away by the other nations. However, He is understanding. G-d knows that His children live a constant struggle against the evil instinct. The evil instinct is a tree planted in the heart of every Jew. When Mashiach will be here, soon in our days, this tree would lose its fruits and leaves.

Haftarah Naso
Judges 13:2-25

Shimshon, the savior of Israel, belonged to the tribe of Dan. His father was Manoach, and his mother was Tzlelponi from the tribe of Yehuda. However, she lived in the land of the tribe of Dan. Both tribes were compared to lions.
Therefore, Shimshon symbolized strength.

A messenger of G-d appeared to Shimshon's mother and said, "You will have a son that will be a Nazir." Immediately, the woman ran to notify her husband. But Manoach did not understand why the messenger
appeared only to his wife.

Manoach prayed to G-d so that the messenger would appear to him too. G-d granted him his wish. Tzelponi ran to inform Manoach about the reappearance of the messenger. The messenger of G-d explained to Manoach that the message was given to his wife because she was the one who would give birth to the baby.

Shimshon was born and his name came from the word "Shemesh," or "Sun," "G-d is a Sun and a Shield," as is written in the Psalms. Shimshon was touched when he used to see how the Philistines caused Israel so much suffering. His supernatural strength became G-d's way in order to defend his people.

Haftarah Behaalotecha
Zecharia 2:14 – 4:7

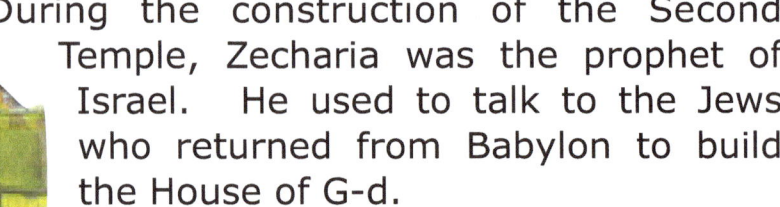

During the construction of the Second Temple, Zecharia was the prophet of Israel. He used to talk to the Jews who returned from Babylon to build the House of G-d.

King Nebuchadnezzar sent three men to the oven: Michael, Chananiah and Azariah. When the king saw them leaving the oven with no skin burns, the three gained so much holiness before the entire community, that they returned to the Land of Israel, and learned the great Torah with Yehoshua, the Kohen Gadol.

Prophet Zecharia instilled in Yehoshua to continue the construction of the Second Temple. In every stone of the construction, seven eyes looked after its conclusion; one for each Jewish leader: Yehoshua, Ezra, Zeruvavel, Nechamia, Chagai, Zecharia and Malachi.

Finally, the Second Temple was finished in spite of the Kusim who intervened to prevent its completion.

The Second Temple was completed on the sixth year of Darius kingdom. He searched for the consent letter written by Emperor Korech among all the archives, because it permitted the building of the Temple. When it was found, Darius managed to finish the Temple. The people enjoyed great abundance and many invitations to eat from its grapes and figs.

"Neither for number nor for strength, only with the spirit of G-d,"The Second Temple achieved its completion only through divine inspiration, and not because of the strength of Zeruvavel who was the political leader of the time.

Haftarah Shelach Lecha
Yehoshua 2:1-24

The city of Jericho was blocked and if the Jews had conquered it, it would had been under their control. Yehoshua, the second leader after Moshe, sent Pinchas and Kaleb to explore the land.  The main reason was in order to save Rahab, a soul who yearned to be Jewish. Rahab had just become fifty when she discovered G-d, the True One. She learned who is G-d when she heard about the victory of Israel after the war with Sichon and Og.

This is how Pinchas and Kaleb saved Rahab from the city of Jericho following G-d's instructions. Rahab protected them from the guards, and found them the best hiding place. She hid them on the roof of her house covered with sticks of linseed. Rahab declared her faith in G-d to them, and her wish to be part of the people of Israel. Rahav was a convert who accepted the Torah just as Tziporah, Ruth and Hagar did.

One of the walls of Rahab's house was also part of the wall of Jericho. She helped Pinchas and Kaleb escape through this wall.

Pinchas and Kaleb promised Rahab that she will be saved the day of the conquest of Jericho. She would have to tie a red string in the window as a sign, and hide all of her relatives inside her house. Everyone would be saved if they observed the Seven Mitzvoth of Noach.

G-d ordered Yehoshua Bin Nun to marry Rahab. Her name in Hebrew means "wide." The meaning of her name gave Rahab the merit to have many descendants, that could marry Kohanim.

If Rahab and Yitro, Moshe's father in law, both converts, knew G-d, one who was born a Jew could know Him too. All of us can serve G-d throughout prayer, learning, and kindness. Our profession is not a reason to let go of our service to G-d with sincerity.

Haftarah Korach
Samuel I 11:14 – 12:22

On the one hand, the people of Israel distanced themselves from the Judges. They asked prophet Samuel for a king like the rest of the nations. Samuel prayed to G-d, and a stream of water fell in the middle of the drought.

Prophet Samuel spoke to the people of Israel in his old age, saying, "For what do you need a king if you have G-d, King of Kings?" "He can do everything."

Then, Samuel prayed to G-d for the rain. Immediately, G-d sent a downpour. The people thought, "Everything that the prophet asks for, is given." This made them understand that it was not necessary to request a king. They had Samuel, the prophet, who could save them from any risk.
Samuel promised them that G-d would never abandon them.

On the other hand, Korach and company distanced themselves from Moshe and Aaron. When Korach be sorry about so grave a sin, he would flourish like a palm tree in the years to come.

Haftarah Chukat
Judges 11:1-33

Gilad from the tribe of Menashe married a concubine. He had a son whom he named Yiftach. After, he got married again but this time, with a more refined woman. He had more children with her second wife.

Yiftach was the firstborn of Gilad. However, his brothers gave him a dirty look because he was a son of a concubine. He did not even protested because he loved peace, especially between his siblings. Yiftach preferred to separate from them and left the land of Israel.

After a short while, the elders of Israel went to get Yiftach to bring him back to Israel. "We need you to lead the war against the Amonites," they told him.
First, Yiftach prayed to G-d. Later, he spoke with the Amonites to see if they could solve the problem peacefully. But he was not successful and the war against the Amonites started. G-d gave strength and courage to Yiftach
from the beginning to the end of the war.

What does Yiftach teach us? A leader has to set a time for the study of Torah.

While Eisav was not learning Torah, Yaakov Avinu spent his time in Torah learning since birth. Yaakov and Torah are one. The angel of Eisav who attacked him, knew that the Torah guarantees the existence of Israel.

Haftarah Balak
Micah 5:6 – 6:8

Prophet Micah spoke to the people of Israel saying, "You would have pure trust in G-d in Mashiach times." "You would be like the dew and the rain for the other nations." "This would bring blessing to the world."

Micah continued, "the Finger of G-d had rescued human beings in various times. His Thumb and His Hand would be used to show His Strength in the future." G-d wrote the Ten Commandments with His Finger. And also with His Finger He attacked the Egyptians.

Micah taught the people of Israel to find G-d. He said to them, "The Torah teachers are like the mountains, great guides of the community." The Torah students and the righteous people are smaller mountains that show the way to others too."

At the same time that generations passed, the spiritual level of the Jews weakened. King David mentioned ten duties. Prophet Isaiah mentioned six.

Prophet Micah focused on three: Honesty between man and his neighbor, Acts of kindness, and Modesty before G-d in practice and thought.

Haftarah Pinchas
Kings I 18:46 – 19:21

The most idol worshiping of all the kings was king Ahab. Once, prophet Eliyahu offered a sacrifice on the Carmel mountain and burned all the idols. At this moment, the Jews declared, "G-d is the True G-d."

When queen Jezebel realized what Eliyahu had done, he escaped. The prophet arrived at the Sinai desert and sat down under a broom tree. After having eaten a piece of broiled bread, Eliyahu fell asleep under the tree. G-d wanted to wake him up so that he would pray for the Chosen People.

When G-d said to Eliyahu to pray for the people, he had to do it calmly and quietly. G-d does not reveal himself in a fuss, in the wind or in the fire. On the contrary, G-d wants to listen to soft sounds with love and good words. In this way, the people could return to Him with integrity.

However, prophet Eliyahu did not pay attention to the people's merits. This is why G-d did not let him pray for their benefit. Then, G-d said to Eliyahu, "Go and find someone else to take up your place." Prophet Eliyahu found Elisha who was his student. Because Elisha put up with the sins of the people, he helped them return to G-d.

Haftarah Matot
Jeremiah 1:1 -2:3

Prophet Jeremiah transmitted G-d's messages in the Jerusalem's streets and markets. Jeremiah descended from Rahab, the woman who saved Kaleb and Pinchas, the spies whom Yehoshua sent to Jerico.

Jeremiah spoke to the people using reprimands. His goal was to motivate the people of Israel to abandon the idols, and be closer to G-d. In reality, Jeremiah did not want to be the spokesperson of sermons and bad news. He did not want to accept this divine mission. Then, G-d promised him He would watch over his tranquility.

Prophet Jeremiah's goal was to motivate the people of Israel to abandon the idols, and be closer to G-d.

Haftarah Masei
Jeremiah 2:4-28, 3:4, 4:1-2

The children of Israel came from a strong foundation, from the patriarcs Abraham, Isaac and Jacob. They seem like sweet wine. When the children of Israel don't trust in G-d, they look like Eisav and Yishmael.
They resemble a strange wine.

In the time in which prophet Jeremiah reprimanded the children of Israel, his messages were also directed to all of humanity. Jeremiah used to say.
"Everybody has to pay attention to G-d and follow His Pathways." G-d is the "Aluf Neurai," the Mentor of Youth, Who accompanies the children of Israel along the way of good deeds and Who teaches Israel to get close to Him.

Prophet Jeremiah used to say: "Everybody has to pay attention to G-d and *follow His Pathways.*"

Book of Devarim
Deuteronomy

Haftarah Devarim

Isaiah 1:1-27

In the Hebrew language, the word "prophesy" is translated as "nebuah." In addition to "nebuah," there are nine other words with the same meaning. Three of them are: chazon, masa and deebur. Chazon, which means vision, is the highest level of prophesy.

Prophet Isaiah was born in Jerusalem from an important family. His father was prophet Amotz. Isaiah was a very humble person in spite of his agressiveness during his conversations with G-d. Isaiah lived 120 years.

The vision of Isaiah had reminded the Jews to return to G-d. He reprimanded them because they did not think good thoughts. When they stole, their hands became impure; when they complained before G-d, He responded them with silence.

Prophet Isaiah explained to the Jews that by being honest, they would avoid punishment. If they are just, straight and sincere, the salvation would soon come. Justice is a sign of the Torah; being straigh is Israel's essence. Both protect the people from any shortage.

Prophet Isaiah explained to the Jews that by being honest, they would avoid punishment.

Haftarah Vaetchanan
Isaiah 20:1-26

G-d said to the prophets to comfort the people of Israel. He said the word "comfort" twice, stressing it. Why? The first "comfort" was for those who saw the the destruction of Jerusalem. The second "comfort" would be for the future generations in the time of the final redemption.

Prophet Isaiah said, "the grass dies and the flowers wither, but the word of G-d is forever." In other words, the nations without morals had been like the grass that dies, but G-d's salvation would be forever.

The true payment has always been to be with G-d: learning about Creation, living with the Tradition and recognizing Him as the Creator of Universe. In the future redemption, the children of Israel would be like stars. They would travel to Jerusalem and be comforted.

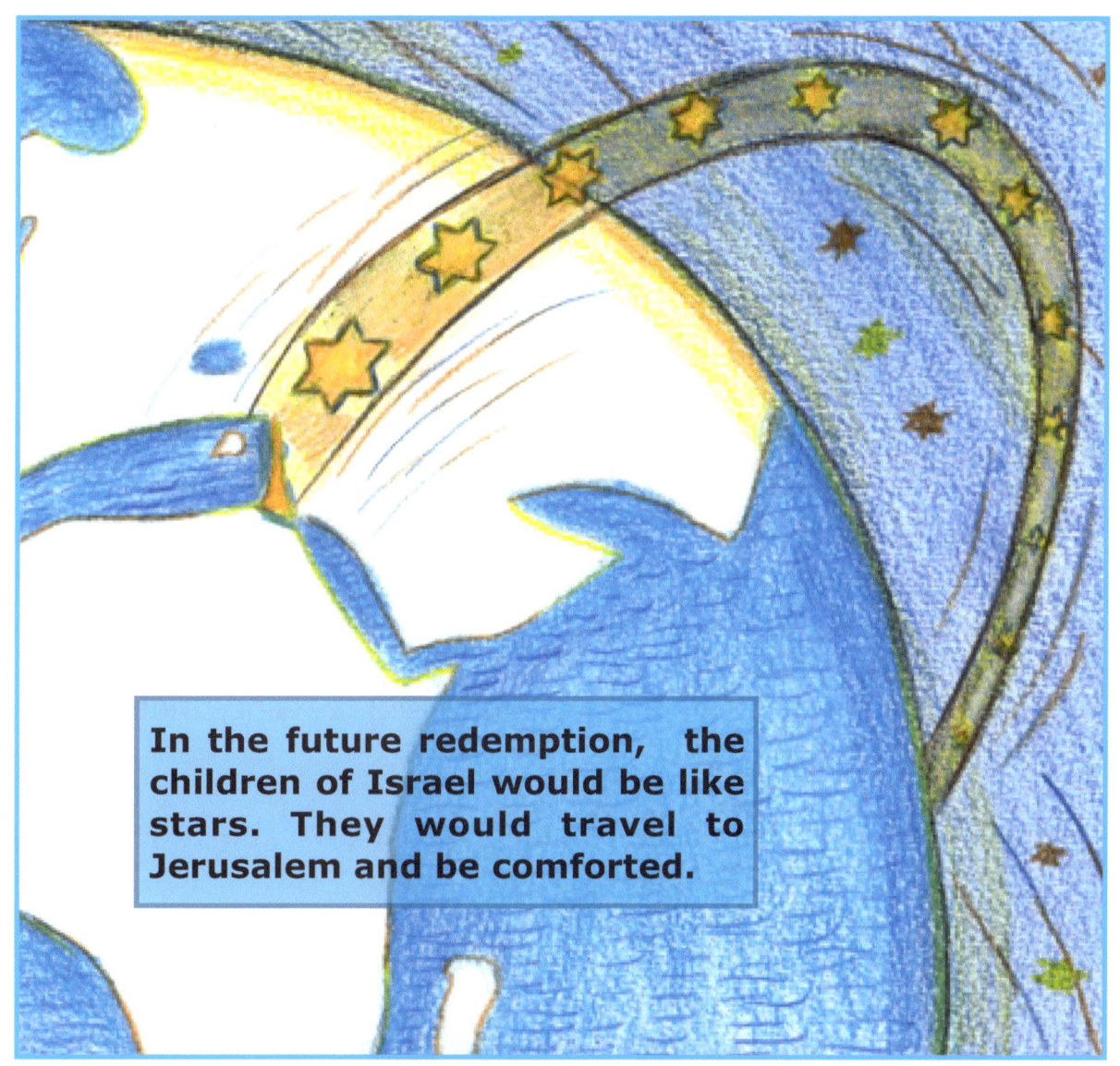

In the future redemption, the children of Israel would be like stars. They would travel to Jerusalem and be comforted.

Haftarah Ekev
Isaiah 49:14 -51:3

The Jewish nation was known with many names; one of them is Tzion represented by a woman. The mother Tzion always worried about the physical and spiritual well-being of Israel. Tzion has been the holiest place in the city of Jerusalem as well.

G-d has taken care of the Jewish nation in the whole world. The Jewish nation has been the lonely sheep among seventy wolves. Each wolf symbolized one nation. This relationship was an expression of divine compassion because the Jewish communities, scattered around the seventy nations, will never disappear.

In the time of the redemption, G-d will give the other nations free permits for the Jews to exit their territories, and will provide them with the means to travel to the Promised Land.

the Jewish communities, scattered around the seventy nations, will never disappear

Haftarah Ree
Isaiah 54:11 – 55:5

The Midrash teaches us about a Jewish boy who traveled in a sinking ship. He had a precious stone in his hands. The name of the special stone was Kadkod. G-d saved the boy and he managed to survive.

The boy went to Rabbi Yehoshua Ben Levi to show him the stone. The meeting was private. The Rabbi observed how the kadkod illuminated the whole city. The boy was thankful the the Rabbi took the time to examine the stone. As the lad was walking outside, he threw the stone on the soil, and it stayed there until today.

The Kadkod is the stone that will decorate Jerusalem in the time of Mashiach. In the same way that the Kadkod illuminated the Holy City, the Torah will shine in the minds of the Jews. They will not forget their learning, and will remember their traditions. Peace will reign, and all the misunderstandings and discussions will stay in the back.

Haftarah Shoftim

Shoftim 51:12-52:12

Fear to the enemy will disappear when the Jews meditate and fear G-d.

Israel left Egypt in a rush. Then, G-d divided the Red Sea to teach them the danger to walk over the sea waves. G-d was the Only Who could calm the furious waves that scared the people of Israel so much.

The people's sins do not allow the world to become pure. Therefore, G-d sends "two angels" to purify the world: "The sages" and "the children," who learn the Torah and recite the Shema Israel. The world refines itself and hope is rekindled.

The people of Israel is distributed over the whole world. This benefits the Jewish communities all over the globe. For they will help each other in difficult times, and in this way, the Jewish communities will survive.

Haftarah Ki Tetze

Isaiah 54:1-10

The Jews are dispersed over the entire world, however they will be gathered in Jerusalem with the arrival of Mashiach. Even though G-d will decree that Jerusalem be expanded, the holliness of the city will keep up its charming appeal for residents, travelers and visitors.

G-d will cause a rise in Jewish population, in the same way as when they were slaves in Egypt. Delivering many children to the world contributes to the arrival of Mashiach. The Gemara teaches that every Jewish soul should descend from the Heavenly Treasure, down to this world, before Mashiach present himself.

The humility of Noach was so great, that he was not able to believe his mission to save the world from the flood. Even though Noach built the Ark, he did not pray for the people to return to G-d. As a result, our sages taught to pray **in the first person plural** because we should always pray for all, including us.

Haftarah Ki Tavo

Isaiah 60:1-22

Today, the Jew cannot communicate directly with G-d. His lack of faith and experience diverts him from the path of truth. In the midst of this lack of awareness, a small light beam illuminates him: The light of the Torah.

Jerusalem, the lamp that illuminates the world, will be the spiritual capital, and all the kings will join the Jews in their return to the land of Israel. The kings will help them to rebuild their cities. Peace will reign.

The kingdom of Mashiach will work without problems and injustices. The sun and the moon will not stop shining. G-d's light will be brighter than all the others.

Haftarah Nitzavim

Isaiah 61:10-63-9

A person's dress express his character. G-d's attire has taught Israel to discover His qualities.

When G-d appears dressed in white, He has pardoned Israel's sins. Moreover, when He appears dressed in red, He presents Himself with justice, as of when the Edomites caused Israel so much suffering.

While the color white represents mercy, the red symbolizes justice. Israel's deliverance will be like the dress of the bride and groom: white.

Haftarah Vayelech

Hoshea 14:2-10; Yoel 2:11-27; Micah 7:18-20

Prophet Hoshea said to Israel to "take" the words seriously. The Jews did not understand how can they "take" the words. Then, the prophet explained to them, that the words are sounds of prayer.

They wanted to understand a little better and asked the prophet again. He told them, "When you dedicate a few moments before prayer sincerely, and take your words seriously with concern, then, you will walk along the path of good deeds."

The children of Israel are compared to the dew when they return to G-d. They are compared to a rose that opens its petals when they study the Torah. They are compared to the roots of the cedar from Lebanon when they do Teshuva.
Neither Israel nor the cedar tree are moved by the fury of the winds. G-d will forever supply the children of Israel with water as He did with the grass.

Prophet Micah said, "A humble person does not admit that his sins will be forgiven." Prophet Joel said, "G-d wishes that a person control his heart." What did the prophets mean with their words? A person should eliminate the acts of selfishness and arrogance because these deviate him from the truth.

Haftarah Haazinu

Samuel 22:1-41

When David was saved from the hand of King Saul, he dedicated a song of thanks to G-d. David was characterized by his Humility, Torah and Strength. He carried the Holy Ark to Jerusalem without arrogance. When he was declared king by prophet Samuel, he was not arrogant. And, he always felt like a newborn who depended on his mother.

David asked G-d that his name be included in the Amida prayer together with Abraham, Isaac and Yaakov. G-d's answer was negative. "Why?" David asked Hashem. He said that whereas David did not pass the test with Batsheva, Abraham, our father, passed the ten tests.

After David made Teshuva, he asked G-d again to include him in the Amida prayer. G-d did not accept, but He included David's name in the blessings of the haftarah, when we say the "Shield of David". David thanked G-d for having saved him from so many dangers. In the same way, the Jewish people thank G-d for having saved them from all circumtances.

We say the word "Magdil," in the weekday's Birkat Hamazon, the blessing after eating a meal with bread. "Magdil" means "to increase." However, we pronounce "Migdol" in the Shabbat's Birkat Hamazon. Why? "Migdol" means that "increased enough." During the week, we increase spiritually. On Shabbat we reach the tip of the mountain in our spirituality. "Migdol" corresponds to the taste of the world to come, a constant Shabbat.

Haftarah Bezot Haberach
Yehoshua 1:1-18

When Moshe passed on, Yehoshua was declared the new leader of Israel. G-d taught him that the success of the Jewish people depends on every person who lives a life of Torah. G-d prepared him to be strong and persistent, Chazak Veematz, in spite of life's difficulties.

During the leadership of Yehoshua, G-d defined the boundaries of the land of Israel. To the south, the Zin Desert; to the north, with Lebanon; to the northeast with the Eufrates River; and to the west with the Mediterranean Sea.

Whereas Moshe took the Jews out of Egypt, Yehoshua brought them to Canaan, which is Israel. Moshe divided the Red Sea and Yehoshua separated the Jordan River. Both stopped the sun temporarily.

G-d said to Yehoshua that the Torah should always be studied. Each Jew should observe it by Pronouncing its words, Pondering on them, Putting them into practice.

G-d also adviced Yehoshua that each Jew should strengthen himself in the Learning of Torah, Prayers, Acts of Kindness and his Profession. Likewise, G-d communicated Yehoshua that the fifth book of the Torah, Devarim, will not be abandoned. Thus, Yehoshua studied this book when G-d talked to him. It is recommended that the Jewish kings and leaders learn the book of Devarim, because it contains laws and teachings about going to war and making judgements.

> G-d communicated Yehoshua that the fifth book of the Torah, Devarim, will not be

Yehoshua sent a messenger to the other side of the Jordan River, where the tribes of Reuven, Gad and part of Menashe lived. His mission was to remind them that their men should join the rest of the tribes in the other side to give them moral and military support during wars. Their wives could stay in their homes. Reuven, Gad and half of Menashe answered, "Like so should it be done."

THE LAST WORD

In the book of Devarim chapter 30, verse 3, it says, "G-d will gather all the Jewish people spread among the nations of the world, and will return them to the land of Israel".

> in any moment we have to leave EVERYTHING and return to the Promise Land.

Most of the haftarot of the five books of the Torah, are about the future deliverance of Israel. Our sages teach that the Jew can't lose hope about the future redemption.

The Midrash advices not to build sophisticated and luxurious houses because they give the impression of wanting to remain in the Diaspora. Thus, the future Redemption alerts each Jew that in any moment he has to leave EVERYTHING and return to the Promise Land.

Haftarot of the Jewish Holidays and Fasts days

Haftarah First Day of Rosh Hashanah
Samuel I 1:1 - 2:10

Hashgacha Peratit (Divine Providence) is everything that happens to us because of G-d's plan. By means of the Tefillah (Prayer) we dedicate to Him and we focus on G-d's control of our lives. Therefore, destiny can be changed by G-d because of our Tefillah.

Chana, mother of the prophet Samuel, and our mothers Sara and Rachel, prayed and G-d changed their destiny so that they could have good children. The main theme of Rosh Hashana is Hashgacha Peratit. The Haftarah focuses on Chana's destiny, and her husband Elkana, who was a great sage from Korach's family. Elkana was also married to Penina, who gave birth to ten children, but Chana was not able to give birth. Chana felt anxious because Penina bothered her for not a able to have children. Commentaries say that Penina bothered Chana so that she would pray deeply to Hashem. Either way, a person can't cause another one such a heavy pain.

We are all children of G-d. He feels our pain in the same way as He felt Chana's pain when she expressed her feelings heartfully. Chana promised G-d that her son would serve Him his entire life, and that he will be a nazir.

Praying deeply to G-d may be seen as unreasonable by some of the people who look at us. When Eli, the Cohen Gadol, saw Chana begging to Hashem in Shilo, he thought she was drunk. Chana explained to him the reason of her prayers, and Eli blessed her so that Hashem would give her a son. Samuel, Chana's son, whom she prayed to G-d so much for, was born in the seventh month, on Rosh Hashanah. Chana nurtured him for two years, and then, she and her husband brought him to Shilo to thank Hashem. Chana's song is the best song of thanks to G-d for giving birth to a child.

G-d knows everything that will happen, and everything depends on Him. This is Hashgacha Peratit. He wants us to communicate our feelings to Him because we are His children and He wishes us only good.

Haftarah for the second day of Rosh Hashanah
Jeremiah *31:1-19*

The Haftarah revolves around the theme of future redemption. The prophet Yirmiyahu assures the people of Israel that G-d wants them, and in the future will redeem them by returning them to the Land of Israel. The redemption process will slow down for the weak and disabled so that they will be able to get ahead with the rest of the Jews.

Rachel, our mother, gave her sister Leah and her concubines, everything she had. Because of her humility and kindness, G-d rewarded Rachel with two sons, Yosef and Binyamin.

The children of Israel are characterized by their humility. For this reason, they are also called Ephrayim. This name comes from the Hebrew word "Efer," ashes, which is equal to humility. Even if Ephrayim (Israel) would not return to Hashem, He will love them forever. However, if Ephrayim does return to Hashem, He will love them like His own son. The love between Hashem and Ephrayim is infinite, since the Jews declared in Mount Sinai, "We will do and we will listen."

The nations of the world will listen to the news about the Redemption. Everybody will understand that the reason behind the dispersion of the children of Israel for so many years was to eventually bring them to the Land of Israel. Only one button needs to be pressed to activate the Redemption. The button's name is Teshuva. When the children of Israel returns to G-d, the button will be activated.

Haftara Shacharit Yom Kippur

Isaiah 57:14 - 58:4

The prophet Yeshayahu warns the children of Israel to remove the obstacles from their lives. These are the Yetzer Hara. In the future, Hashem will come to the children of Israel to clear the paths of these obstacles.

The purpose of Yom Kippur is to improve the traits of each one of the children of Israel by way of Teshuva. The fast day of Yom Kippur is an opportunity to start anew and become a better person.
The prophet Yeshayahu points out the ways for personal improvement: among others, sanctifying the Shabbat and helping the poor.

Several practices used to help a poor person are giving him food, a roof, and clothing. The one who gives should encourage the poor person with his words and with his heart. Therefore, he will acquire a good name and his reward will be complete.
When one observes the Shabbat correctly, it is as if he keeps the Torah entirely. Every word that is mentioned in Shabbat, should be related to the holiness of the day.

Haftara Mincha Yom Kippur
Book of Yona

As we said before, the purpose of Yom Kippur is to improve our behavior. Hashem called Yona, the prophet, in order to destroy Nineveh from evil people. However, the prophet refused to obey Hashem's will.

When Yona was a child, he was awakened by prophet Eliyahu in a widow's house. Hashem ordered him to destroy Nineveh with all of its people because they did not want to return to Him. Yona then refused to obey in order to protect Israel.

Yona left the land of Israel to escape G-d's decree. He paid the ticket to all the sailors: 4,000 dinars. The ship sailed to Tarshish that is believed to be in Africa.

Hashem did not let Yona live in peace and He sent a great sea storm. The ship moved tempestuosly. The sailors prayed to their gods. Yona did not pray because he was sure that the storm was sent by G-d. The sailors noticed that Yona was the main reason why the storm happened. Then, little by little, they threw him to the sea and it became peaceful again.

The only thing that Hashem wanted was that Yona would understand that His decree needed to be kept. Hashem sent Yona a giant fish to swallow him so he would fulfill the Divine will. Hashem's goal was to make Yona reconsider the mission to destroy Nineveh. Hashem did not want to harm Yona at any moment. When Yona felt very comfortable inside the fish, he did not pray to Hashem. So Hashem sent him the third test to be swallowed by another fish. In this one, Yona felt very uncomfortable, and thus, he began to pray to Hashem and become close to Him. Yona was very sure that Hashem would save him.

Then Yona decided to keep the decree. He traveled to Nineveh for three days. The king of Nineveh warned his people that no one could steal. Yona thought that this was a false repentance. For Hashem even the smallest effort to erase the sin of robbery was not superficial, like Yona had thought. Hashem requires an honest and sincere return from the nations of the world. However, Hashem expects a relationship, which is closer, deeper, and of a higher category from the children of Israel. The teshuva of Yona purified him from his negativity, and made him closer to Hashem <u>with humility</u>.

Haftara First Day of Succoth
Zecharia 14:1-21

The Haftara is about the War of Gog and Magog. All the nations of the world will attack Jerusalem, and at the end of the war during the holiday of Succoth, they will visit the Beth Hamikdash. The nations will trust Hashem and they will know that He is the Only G-d.

The prophet Zecharia says that the nations will attack the descendants of Edom, Ashur, and Yishmael. The children of Israel will be confused because they won't know what the result of the war will be.

Hashem will be the Main Actor of the war against the nations. This war will develop in the time before Mashiach, who will come to redeem them in the future. Hashem will be the Only Authority. Hashem will reunite all the nations in Jerusalem for Israel's own good. The children of Israel will collect the riches of Gog's army.

In the future, during the holiday of Succoth when the children of Israel will bless the four species, Hashem will bring rain to the land of Israel. The rain will depend on their merits, which are the mitzvoth of moral intergrity.

Haftara Second Day of Succoth
Kings I 8:2-21

The Haftara is about the dedication of the First Beit Hamikdash during the Kingdom of Shlomo. Being that the inauguration was held before Succoth, this is the Haftarah for the second day of the festival.

The Beit Hamikdash was a two story building where Hashem decided to reside. It was finished on 2935 after seven years and a half. The holy objects of the Beit Hamikdash were the same that where used in the Mishkan, except the Aron. This one was the holiest object and therefore, it was forbidden to duplicate. It was moved from place to place until King David put it inside a tent in Jerusalem.

The inauguration was a spectacular, seven day ceremony. The Levites sang, the Kohanim carried the Aron, and King Shlomo and his retinue of 1000 Jews marched in front of the Aron.

When they arrived to the Beit Hamikdash, they placed the Aron in the Dvir, which was the holiest site of the Temple. The doors of the Dvir did not open, and King Shlomo assumed that it was because of his father David's sin. The Beit Hamikdash had the power to forgive any Jew's sin. Thus, when King Shlomo pronounced the name of King David, the doors of the Dvir opened and his sin was forgiven.

The Aron was placed in the middle of the Dvir, and the Divine Presence resided in the Beit Hamikdash from that moment on.

King Shlomo thanked Hashem for having given him the opportunity to build the Beit Hamikdash. Although King Shlomo built it, his father David received the complete reward. What a great honor was it to build the

Haftara Shabbat Chol Hamoed Succot

Ezekiel 30:18 - 39:16

There is a Midrash that says that the fall of Gog will take place on the seventh day of Succoth, which is Hoshana Rabba. From here it is concluded that the fall of Og symbolizes the victory of the Sukkah because it happened during the holiday of Succoth, as prophet Ezekiel prophesied.

Who is Gog? Who is Magog?
Gog will direct the nation of Magog, and Magog is Noach's son Yafet; both are the biggest enemies of Hashem in the world. Anyone who wants to defeat the children of Israel, is automatically an enemy of Hashem.

Gog wants to become independent of Hashem, and build his own roof that will separate him from G-d. Gog wants to show his weapons to invade the Land of Israel, but Hashem will show His true power. The Land of Israel belongs only to the children of Israel. Hashem will punish Gog and his allies with fire. Both will be buried in the Land of Israel. This great mitzvah will bring honor to Hashem. The Jews will get a good name because they devoted themselves to the enemy with compassion and dignity.

The name of the city where Gog and Magog will be buried will be called "Hamona," meaning crowd. Hamona will be an eternal monument where goodness triumphs over evil, and mankind will be close to Hashem

Haftara Shemini Atzeret

Kings I 8:54 - 9:1

The Haftara is about the final days of the inauguration of the Beit Hamikdash by King Shlomo. In the same manner, Shemini Atzeret is the eight and final day of the Succoth holiday.

The inauguration of the Beit Hamikdash was one of the happiest occasions in Jewish history. This House of Hashem would have been everlasting if it hadn't been for a misstep of King Shlomo. Hashem did not approve that the king marry an Egyptian woman. Even though the king had good reasons to do it, Hashem did not like it and therefore, He destroyed the Beit Hamikdash.

King Shlomo prayed to Hashem with outstretched hands loudly for giving him the opportunity to build the Beit Hamikdash. Within seven days after the inauguration, the commemoration of Yom Kippur took place. The Sanhedrin decreed not to fast that day so the inauguration would not be disrupted. At the end of it, the Jews said farewell to the king. Since they decided to stay one more day, the Jews said farewell to the king again.

The inauguration of the first Beit Hamikdash was something unique. For this reason, the Jews stayed one more day. When we mention the phrase "Like in the old days", we are referring to the unforgettable inauguration of the First Beit Hamikdash.

Haftara Simchat Torah

Yehoshua 1:1-18

The Haftara is about the next leader of the children of Israel, Yehoshua. The leadership transition from Moshe to Yehoshua parallels the holiday transition from Simcha Torah to the daily routine of the new year.

- Y ehoshua was characterized by
- E xamining the Torah on a daily basis.
- H ashem considered him His servant. Yehoshua was
- O ccupied with helping Moshe in a personal manner.
- S pecial and outstanding quality of
- H umility made him a vessel for a
- U nique aspect of the Torah.
- A nd we know it as the Oral Torah.

Hashem defined the boundaries of the Land of Israel. From the desert of Zin on the south, to the Lebanon on the east. From the Euphrates river on the northeast to the Land of Chitim, and to the Mediterranean Sea to the west.

The most important advice that Hashem gave Yehoshua was not to distance himself from the teachings of his teacher. These lessons, the Torah, are for the soul of Yehoshua and Israel, in the same way as bread and water are basic to the body. Another advice that Hashem gave Moshe and later to Yehoshua was to be strong and to persevere, in Hebrew, "Chazak veematz." When one perseveres in his work, the obstacles become less difficult.

On the seventh of Nisan of the year 2488, Yehoshua ordered the children of Israel to cross the Jordan River and enter the King's Palace, the Land of Israel.

In between the months of Adar and Nissan, that correspond to the holidays of Purim and Pesach, four additional portions are read in addition to the portion of Shabbat. These are the portions of **Shekalim, Zachor, Para,** and **Parashat Hachodesh.**

Haftara Parashat Shekalim

Reyes II 11:17 - 12:17

Parashat Shekalim is read on Rosh Chodesh Adar or on the Shabbat before Rosh Chodesh Adar. This portion teaches us about the half shekel that had to be donated to the Beth Hamikdash.

The Haftarah of Parashat Shekalim is about how the ambition of power took hold of Athaliah, daughter of King Ahab of the Kingdom of Israel. She did not let the House of David rule. Athaliah killed all the kings except one, her grandson Tzirya. This child survived thanks to the Kohen Gadol Yehoyada. He hid the boy for seven years in the highest floor of the Kodesh Hakodashim. Yehoyaha took him out of hiding after six years and crowned him king. Athaliah, the evil one, was eliminated from the palace.

The boy, Yehoash, reigned in Israel for forty years. The Kohen Gadol saved him and was his spiritual leader. King Yehoash took control to repair the Beit Hamikdash. The Kohanim were not very successful in fundraising for the repairs since the donors could not give major contributions. Then, the king put a box with a hole inside the Beth Hamikdash. In this way, everyone gave what they felt in their hearts.

It was a very good idea to collect money for **the repairs of t he** temple. Yeho**yaha was king** Yehoash's mentor. Everything went well. Howe**ver, when the Kohe**n Gadol passed away, Yehoash's pride aggr**andized, and he elimina**ted the son of his dear mentor Ye**hoyada whose name w**as Zecharia. **The** light of the wisdom of **a spiritual leader enligh**tens u**s to follow** the right

Haftara Parashat Zachor

Samuel I 15:1-34

Parashat Zachor is read on the Shabbat before Purim. The children of Israel are saved from Haman, who is a descendant of Amalek.

The Haftara of this parasha teaches us anew the significance of a teacher or a mentor. Shmuel, the prophet, instructed Shaul, the first king of Israel. Hashem's command to destroy Amalek needed to be taught by Shmuel. During the wars between Israel and Amalek, king Shaul had doubts to erase Amalek completely from the map. King Shaul followed his emotions instead of focusing on Hashem's command.

After the giving of the Torah, the Amalekites did not accept Israel as Hashem's people. The people that negate Israel's existence, negate Hashem's existence as well. For this reason, it is a mitzvah to erase Amalek from the map. Because King Shaul did not keep with this mitzvah, his teacher Shmuel reproached him. King Shaul did not understand his mistake. Shmuel, the prophet, stressed that a Jewish king cannot deviate from Hashem's word.

As a loyal teacher and mentor, Shmuel prayed to Hashem in order to save the king from losing his crown. Hashem listened to Shmuel's prayer and allowed Shaul's family to survive, even though He removed the crown from Shaul. From this moment, the prophet did not see Shaul anymore.
So Shmuel killed Agag, the Amalekite king, in order to keep Hashem's word. Consequently, Haman was born and this caused Amalek's memory to not be entirely erased from the map.

Haftara Parashat Para

Ezekiel 36:16-38

This Haftara is read on the Shabbat before Rosh Chodesh Nissan. Hashem will sprinkle water over the children of Israel after Mashiach's arrival.

The prophet Ezekiel teaches us that the Land of Israel is holy, and does not accept neither sins nor stains. When the Jews sin in the Land of Israel, Hashem exiles them over different nations.

When the children of Israel sin in the Land of Israel, it is no longer fertile. When they correct their sins and return to Hashem, He will send them great blessings and gifts.

This is Hashem's advice to the children of Israel: They should emulate the virtues of the Patriarchs: Abraham, Isaac, and Yaakov. They should study Torah until Hashem hands the Mashiach over to them at the right moment. They should follow Hashem like small lambs until they arrive to the Shepherd's cottage, Jerusalem.

Haftara Parashat Hachodesh

Ezequiel 45:16 - 46:18

The Haftara takes place during the month of Nissan. The children of Israel were liberated from Egypt, and the third Beit Hamikdash will be inaugurated after Mashiach's arrival. The prophet Ezekiel enumerated all the sacrifices that needed to be offered during the third Beit Hamikdash. Because these sacrifices are many more than the ones mentioned in the Torah, the inauguration will be much longer, six months, from Pesach to Succoth.

Every person showed love and respect to the Beit Hamikdash with each step, because the Divine Presence resided in it. If a Jew entered at the northern or southern door of the Beit Hamikdash, he needed to exit from the same door. In this way, one was part of the place. The same rule applies for a synagogue or for a house of study.

In olden times, the children of Israel asked the prophet Shemuel, for a king. He told them that the Only King is Hashem. The king that they asked for is the Prince or Mashiach. The Prince will receive a thirteenth of the lands that the children of Israel will own. He should not accept donations that the children of Israel will give him from their own lands.

One of the names related to the Prince or Mashiach is *Shilo*, which is a contraction from the Hebrew words Shai and Lo. Shai means gift, and Lo means Him. The Prince or Mashiach will received gifts of leaders because they will recognize him as the Prince of the Children of Israel.

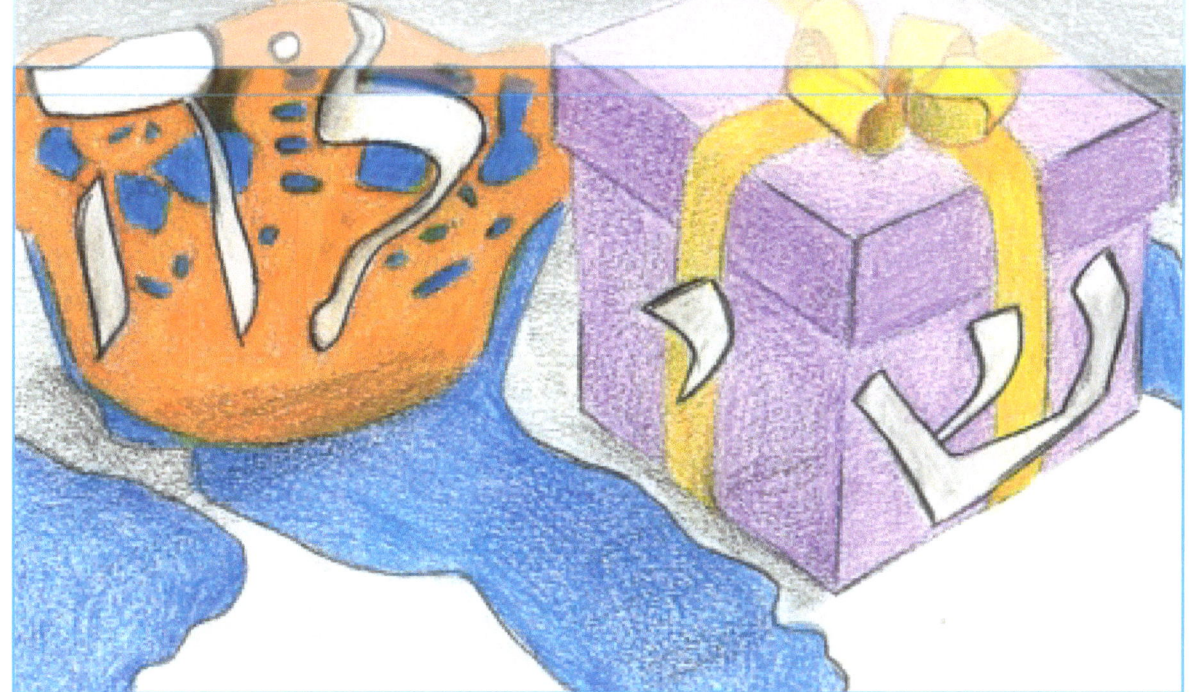

Haftara Shabbat Hagadol
Malachi 3:4-24

This Haftara is read on the Shabbat before Pesach. It is known as the Shabbat Hagadol. Malachi, the last of the prophets, reproached the children of Israel for their lack of enthusiasm when doing mitzvoth. Especially when they did not separate teruma and maaser of ten percent of their earnings. The lack of enthusiasm in observing the mitzvoth of "giving," made the children of Israel live in great poverty. Hashem closed the rain key since they did not donate with enthusiasm. The lack of rain brought a great drought. This caused the children of Israel to think that the drought happened because of scientific reasons. This reasoning prevented them to accept the drought in their own land with faith.

The Great Day of Judgement will be for all the children of Israel in the future, and for each person in particular. The date of the Great Day of Judgement is a mystery. Everything depends on how close Hashem is from the children of Israel. What we know for sure is that before the Day of Judgement, Hashem will send the prophet Eliyahu to strengthen the hearts of every Jew in Torah and in the service of G-d.

The faith that they show with enthusiasm will be recorded in the book of memories. Every effort in the service of Hashem will be rewarded. And those who get attached to the light of the Torah with faith and good attitude, will benefit from the great light in the future. The prophet Malachi's advice is to observe the Torah in its original form, like it was given in Mount Sinai.

Haftara First Day of Pesach

Yehoshua 3:5-7, 5:2, 6:1, 6:27

Moshe, our teacher, parted the Red Sea so that the children of Israel would pass from Egypt into the desert. Yehoshua, his student and successor, parted the Jordan River so that the children of Israel would enter the Land of Israel.

In the desert, the children of Israel had to start obeying Hashem. Yehoshua made the Milah to each baby boy who was eight days old. The Milah symbolizes the pact between Hashem and the children of Israel.

Hashem has five duties with each of His children:
- The Milah or Circumcision
- Pidion Haben or the redemption of the first born
- To Teach him Torah
- To Teach him to observe the mitzvoth
- The blessing of marriage

As the boy grows, he applies the formula or commitment to circumcise and to eliminate the negative in his heart. In other words, the boy must get rid of negative beliefs that contaminate the Milah or pact with G-d.

Yehoshua made the Milah to all the Jewish boys in a place named Gil-Gal. The roots *Gil* and *Gal* come from the verb *Galal*, that means *to remove* in Hebrew. Because both roots are repeated in the word Gilgal, each one represents an aspect of the Milah, removing what is left over.

In the same way that Hashem joined Moshe to take the Jews out of slavery, the angel Michael accompanied Yehoshua to take them to the Land of Israel. The angel Michael told him: Although there is no more "man," and you must work for your livelihood, never overlook the time to study Torah.

The fame of Yehoshua expanded globally. He designed a coin with the image of an ox from both sides. The ox reminded Yehoshua of the blessing that Moshe gave to the tribe of Yosef, to which Yehoshua belonged to. This was the way to show him that he was grateful to his dear teacher, Moshe Rabenu.

Haftara Second Day of Pesach

Kings II 23:1-9, 21:25

The Haftara revolves around the acts of kindness of King Yoshiyahu since he destroyed all the idols of the Land of Israel.

Yoshiyahu was a just king in Israel and Yehuda, who started looking for the G-d of his father David. During that time the evil kings wanted to transform Jerusalem into a city of cults of the Near East. The father and grandfather of Yoshiyahu, Amon and Menashe respectively, introduced idolatry in Israel. However, from age twenty six, Yoshiyahu restored and purified the Beit Hamikdash.

The mission of Yoshiyahu was to return the children of Israel to the service of Hashem, eliminating idolatry from his kingdom. When he succeeded with his mission, Yoshiyahu ordered every Jew in Jerusalem to prepare the Pesach offering in the month of Nissan.

Before king Yoshiyahu, there was no one who returned to Hashem with all his might, soul, and heart.

Yoshiyahu returned to Hashem with pure love. In the same way that the pure originates from the impure, king Yoshiyahu was born from Amon and Menashe respectively.

Haftara Shabbat Chol Hamoed Pesach

Ezekiel 37: 1-14

Hashem commanded Prophet Ezekiel to revive the dead. Techiyat Hametim means the resurrection of the dead in the Hebrew language. According to Jewish tradition, Techiyat Hametim will happen during the holiday of Pesach in the month of Nissan.

The thirteenth principle of faith is to believe that Hashem will resurrect the dead. The person who negates this principle will not be resurrected. The process of revival will start from a bone in the spine that is indestructible.

Three prophets were elected to revive the dead: the prophet Eliyahu, his student Elisha, and the prophet Ezekiel.

Hashem asked Ezekiel, "Will the bones of all the people be resurrected?" The prophet answered, "You'll know." Ezekiel's answer showed the character trait of humility because he ignored the answer. Therefore, he thought that he was not the proper candidate for this mission. At the end, prophet Ezekiel was G-d's messenger to resurrect the dead, and this great miracle revived between 300,000 to 600,000 people.

According to the Torah, death is a prolonged dream. The study of Torah during a person's life will make him acquire the merits to wake up from this dream during Techiyat Hametim. After Mashiach's arrival, the dead will be resurrected, the Beit Hamikdash will be rebuilt, and all the exiled Jews will be together again. AMEN!

Haftara of the Seventh Day of Pesach

Samuel II, I 22:1-51

The Haftara is a Shira (song) that king David dedicated to G-d for having saved him from his enemies. This song that king David wrote is similar to Psalm 18 with some changes.

David thanks Hashem for having saved him from ten enemies: five of whom were Jews, and the other five were not. For each one of them, David writes a title. The following are some of them:

1. G-d is My Rock. The rock that saved him from king Shaul, his first enemy.
2. G-d is the Liberated. The waters of the Red Sea were parted, and the waters of the rivers, lakes, and vessels too. This showed the whole world the miracle of how the children of Israel became free.
3. G-d is the Saviour. Hashem saved David from Achitofel and David's son's Avshalom when they tried to chase David.
4. G-d is the Shield for all those who trust in Him. Hashem protects us constantly from so many dangers, big and small, and we don't even see it.
5. G-d lives. He is the Only Living Being, Independent Forever.

G-d is the Rock of king David Who saved him from death.

G-d is the Rock of each one of His children, who believe that their daily events are always miracles revealed or hidden.

Haftara of the Last Day of Pesach

Isaiah 10:32 - 12:6

King Chizkiyahu prayed with all his heart to Hashem so that Sancheriv, the Assyrian king would not rule over Jerusalem. The children of Israel sang the Hallel to Hashem on that Pesach day in order to praise Him. No prayer is ignored by Hashem and He hears all His children's pleas. He sent the angel Gabriel as the messenger for the miracle of the redemption.

Only G-d knows His miracles, although we may not see them all. We should trust in Him and not be afraid. Because if we trust in Him, and serve Him with joy, He will show us the waters of Torah wisdom.

Mashiach

The Mashiach	....will be able to distinguish between the guilty and the innocent thanks to his elevated spiritual level.
The Mashiach	....will talk and do justice instantly without using arms.
The Mashiach	....will teach 30 mitzvoth instead of the seven mitzvoth of Noach to the other nations.
The Mashiach	....will inspire everybody to obey Hashem in **peace.**

Haftara First day Shavuoth

Ezekiel 1:1-28, 3:12

On the one hand, the children of Israel saw the Divine Presence when they received the Torah of Shavuoth. On the other hand, the prophet Ezekiel discerned the Divine Presence when he visualized the Celestial Throne surrounded by angels.

The Prophet's Vision occurred five years before the people of Israel were exiled from Babylonia. On the fifth of Tamuz, in Babylonia, this vision took place. G-d chose a river as the scenery of the vision because water is pure. The prophet Ezekiel was the only one of the prophets who perceived a vision outside of the Land of Israel. One of the reasons was to ask the Jews when they were going to return to Hashem.

Four creatures were placed beneath the Celestial Chariot: man, the eagle, the ox, and the lion. All four teach us not to be arrogant since G-d Almighty cares for all no matter how great.

According to the Haftara, the glory of G-d is found in the rainbow. For this reason, we should not stare at it for a long time, only for an instant when we are saying its blessing. Because we are not sure where the glory of G-d is, the angels that surround the Celestial Throne teach us to bless Him in His Place, wherever This will be.
That is why we say in the Kedusha of the Amida prayer everyday, "Blessed is the glory of Hashem from **His Place!**

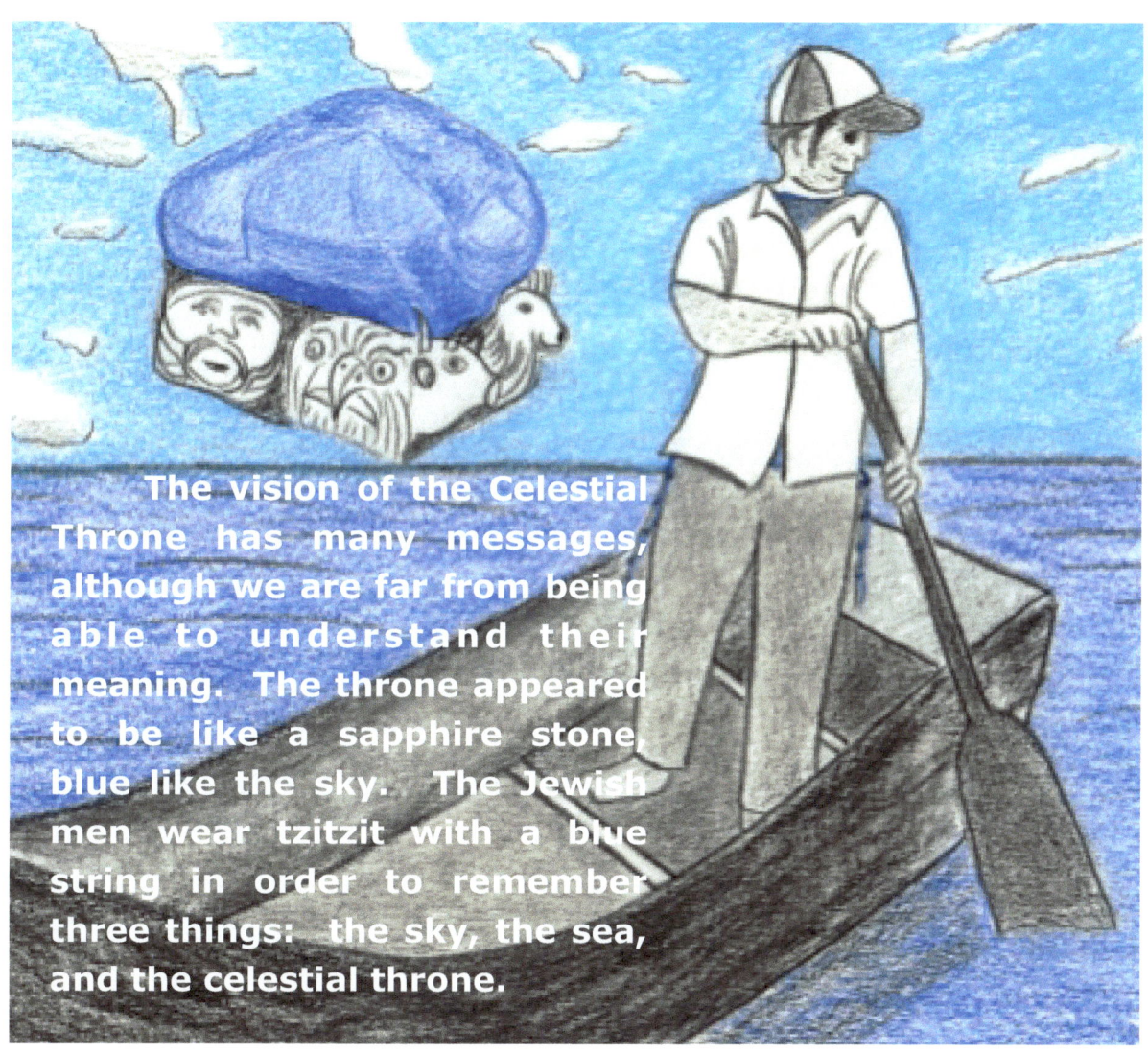

The vision of the Celestial Throne has many messages, although we are far from being able to understand their meaning. The throne appeared to be like a sapphire stone, blue like the sky. The Jewish men wear tzitzit with a blue string in order to remember three things: the sky, the sea, and the celestial throne.

Haftara Second day of Shavuoth

Habakuk 2:20 - 3:19

The prophet Habakuk talked harshly to Hashem because he wanted the exile of the children of Israel to end right away. In the Haftara, the Prophet sings praises to Hashem for the miracles of the conquest and division of the Land of Israel during fourteen years.

The Prophet visualizes the end of the four exiles of the children of Israel when they will be liberated by the Mashiach and revived forever.

The prophet Habakuk asked Hashem in prayer to continue giving life to the Jews so that they will not forget the Torah, the source of their lives. Only through the Torah and the mitzvoth, the Jews could tolerate the darkest moments of their existence.

Only through the Torah and the mitzvoth, the Jews could tolerate the darkest moments of their existence.

Haftara Morning of the Fast of Tisha BeAv
YIrmiyahu 8:13 -9:23

The prophet Yirmiyahu hoped that the Jews of the Land of Israel would hear him, and return to Hashem. The Jews felt far from Hashem until king Nebuchadnezzar of Babylonia invaded Jerusalem. Then, they tried to get close to Hashem, but the king did not let them.

Both Prophet Yirmiyahu and Hashem cried for the suffering of the Jews and for the destruction of Jerusalem. Hashem was the Only One Who knew why the Kingdom of Yehuda fell under the control of Nebuchadnezzar.

The women of Jerusalem demonstrated their consensus for the spiritual and physical loneliness of Jerusalem. Some of them composed songs of lamentations, and others sang them throughout the whole city. In this moment, it was known that the children of Israel would be exiled.

Prophet Yirmiyahu ends by saying that neither the wise, nor the strong or the rich should praise themselves. On the contrary, they should understand that Hashem is kind with those who observe His mitzvoth, and fair with those who get close to Him. In this way, every Jew would be a better person and consequently, the people, a better nation.

The prophet reproached the people because they did not hear the word of Hashem, and turned away from His path. The sins were serious, among them were idolatry, immorality, and speaking evil about others. The third one is like an arrow that once thrown, does not return. The arrow represents the evil commentaries about others and could travel a long distance harming the person whom is being talked about.

Haftara Eve of Rosh Chodesh

Samuel I, 20:18-42

Rosh Chodesh was celebrated with a banquet in honor of the day during the time of the Kings. Because it was Rosh Chodesh, the first day of the month, a special meal was served in honor of the first day of that month. The light of hope illuminated David and his kingdom, every time the moon was renewed in Rosh Chodesh.

When king Shaul met David for the first time, he loved him very much. David's great musical talents and knowledge about Halacha and military strategies, contributed to their friendship. Since G-d removed king Shaul from the throne, he was saddened. His opinion about the young David changed.

Yonatan, the son of Shaul, was very friendly with David. The two forged a friendship pact twice. The second pact was to save Yonatan's descendants.

During the Rosh Chodesh banquet, Yonatan told David to be absent. The two planned a secret way of communication. Like Kohelet says, "A little bird in heaven is calling."

Yonatan informed David to hide in the field for three days behind a rock. When the banquet was over, Yonatan would return to the rock and shoot three arrows. David had to pick an arrow and return it to Yonatan.

DAVID

Yonatan spoke good about his father Shaul, and he also spoke well about his friend David. Yonatan did not want to gossip about anyone especially about the two dearest people in his life. Gossip is compared to an arrow that is directed against the person spoken about. Yonatan did not want to gossip about either his father or friend. Therefore, he used the arrows to communicate with David because talking about others generates three misfortunes: to the speaker, to the listener, and to the one spoken about. On the one hand, Shaul spoke evil about David, and on the other hand, Yonatan spoke good about his father Shaul.

Yonatan was the heir of his father Shaul's throne. However, he saved his friend David, future king of Israel, from the clutches of his own father. Yonatan is a hero worthy of emulation, who reached the highest qualities that a human being can acquire.

Haftara Shabbat Rosh Chodesh

Isaiah 66:1-24

Rosh Chodesh is a small holiday every first day on the month when the moon renews itself.

Shabbat and Rosh Chodesh will be festive days to sanctify Hashem in the future all over the world.

The purpose of Rosh Chodesh is to recognize, even more, the Creator of the World. Rosh Chodesh is also a mitzvah. A mitzvah is not only a commandment, but an opportunity to express our compromise with Hashem. When we do a mitzvah, we do not expect anything in return, but strengthen our relationship with G-d in a true and humble way.

When all the Jews return to Hashem, the exiles of the world will be reunited suddenly and quickly. The Jews will go back to Jerusalem as when the husband returns to his wife after many years. The joy will reign in Jerusalem. The Jews will be so happy, like children nurtured by their mother. They will enjoy peace in the rebuilt Jerusalem.

Hashem will comfort the Jews and only the good will rule within them. When Mashiach will come, soon in our days, the nations' leaders will give him gifts. Hashem will cause these leaders to provide the Jews with means of transportation to bring them to Jerusalem.

Haftara Shabbat Chanukah

Zecharia 2:14, 4:7

Prophet Zecharia visualizes the golden Menorah of the Beth Hamikdash. This prophecy motivated Yehoshua, the Kohen Gadol, and Zeruvavel, the governor, to continue the rebuilding of the Beth Hamikdash.

There were groups, such as the Cusim that prevented the rebuilding. The Cusim were converts to Judaism. Even so, they continued to worship idols. In spite of having prevented the rebuilding of the Beit Hamikdash, the Jews trusted in Hashem that they would be able to finish it.

In the same way that the vision of the Menorah had enough oil, the building of the Second Beit Hamikdash was blessed by the spirit of G-d.

"Not only for the strength (of the Cusim), but for the spirit of Hashem the building of the Second Beit Hamikdash was finished.

Brief Information about Each Prophet

Moses is the Prophet of Prophets. For the sake of this work we are only focusing on the prophets from the Book of Prophets and Biblical Writings because from them the haftarot were taken.

Devorah, the Neviah
Modest

Prophesied……………………2654—2694
(40 years)

Who…………………………..Third of the 7 prophetesses

Husband………………………Barak Ben Avinoam

Personality……………………When speaking to the people, sat under a palm tree to avoid reclusion with men.

Accomplishments……………Blessed those who love Hashem be like the strength of the rising sun.

Elisha Ben Shafat
Disciples

Who?......................................Son of Shafat
                                          Led the Jewish Nation for more than 60 years.

Main Disciple........................Yehoyadah HaKohen

Main Teacher.......................Eliyahu

Teachings............................We only accept gifts with the realization the
                                            it is only G-d the One Who controls the world.
                                            Serving a Torah Sage is better than Torah learning.

Personality...........................Careful not to look at women.
                                            Described as a holy person
                                            Poured water on the hands of Eliyahu
                                            Accepted favors from others

Miracles...............................Were performed through prayer
                                            There were always disciples at his table before and after a meal.

Eliyahu HaNavi
Strictness

Who?.................................One of 8 distinguished leaders in history
His name, Eliyahu, contains the name of G-d in past, present and future. According to the Talmud, he was one of 9 who entered Gan Eden alive.
He is known with 4 names: Yaareshyah, Eliyahu, Zichri and Yerucham. According to Tradition, Pinchas is Eliyahu

Main Disciple........................Elisha

Main Teacher.......................Achiya Ben Shiloni

Personality..........................His approach was with strictness.
Miracles.............................Performed 8 major miracles:
Stopped rain, performed the miracle of the oil, gave life, pray for rain, put the fire down, fasting, splitted the Jordan River. According to Tradition, he will announce the coming of Mashiach, Soon In Our Days!

Elkanah
Man of Hashem

Who?...........................Father of Prophet Samuel
Man Of Hashem (Title given to a prophet)

Wife............................Hannah

Where from?..................Ramahtayim Tzofim

Personality....................Helped people do Teshuvah
Man of Hashem
Resembled Avraham Avinu

Accomplishments............Inspired people to go to the Mishkan in Shilo 3 times a year
Great prophet of the Jewish people during the period of the Judges

Hannah
Power of Prayer

Who?..............................Samuel's mother
Elkanah's wife
First to call Hashem "Master of Hosts"

Teachings..........................We learn the laws of prayer from Hannah.
From the 3 letters of her name in Hebrew, women are reminded to do 3 mitzvoth: **H**allah, **N**idah (laws of family purity), **H**adlakat Ner (lighting Shabbat candles).
Recognized Hashem's power of Creation

Accomplishments................ Prayed for an average child instead for a gifted one in order to avoid the evil eye.
Gave birth on Rosh Hashanah

Challenges........................Childless of 19 years

Hoshea Ben Be'eiri
Repentance

Who?................................Son of Be'eiri
  One of the 12 prophets of Trei Asar
  Contemporary of Yeshaya, Amos and
  Michah

Tribe................................Reuven

Main Disciple......................Amos

Main Teacher......................Zecharia

Teachings..........................First to teach about repentance.

Main Prayer.......................I will betroth You to me forever.

Book...............................Book of Hoshea consists of 14
  chapters.

AMEN!

Huldah
Power of Amen

Who?.................................6th. of the 7 prophetesses
Wife of Shalum Ben Tikvah
She prophesied for the women while Yirmiyahu prophesied for the men.

Personality..........................Huldah was more learned in Torah
The Gates of Huldah were built so that she would teach and guide the people there.

Teachings............................One who listens to a blessing and responds Amen, is considered as the one who has said the blessing himself. Not necessary for us to be primary participants of the mitzvah.

Accomplishments..................Husband and wife relationship is a team that benefits both of them.
Her husband Shalum gave hope to others, and as a result of his kindness, Huldah became a prophetess.

Malachi
Emissary

Who?.............................According to the Gemara,
                                 Malachi was really Ezra.
                                 Was the last prophet.
                                 The name Malachi means "My Emissary."

Main Function....................Torah teacher.

Legacy...........................Initiated the transition between the time of the prophets and the Torah Sages.

Teaching.........................According to the Talmud, we should always learn Torah from our Sages because they are the angels of Hashem. A prophet is called angel because he is always close to Hashem.

Book.............................The Book of Malachi is the 12th. section Trei Asar. Consists of 3 chapters.

Michah
Mercy

Who?...............................Called Michah of Morashah

Main Disciple......................Yoel

Main Teacher.....................Yeshaya

Teachings..........................The 13 Principles of Mercy
                                        Torah = Justice + Kindness + Modesty

Book............................... The Book of Michah consists of 7 chapters. Michah is the 6th book of Trei Asar.

Ovadyah
Devotion

Who?.............................One of 12 prophets in the Book of Trei Asar. The name Ovadyah means a devoted servant of Hashem. Ovadyah was a convert from Edom.

Personality........................Ovadyah became great and righteous.

Main Task..........................To rebuke Edom

Challenge...................... Even though Ovadyah lived among the evil queen Izevel and king Achav, he feared Hashem. Ovadyah spent all his money to sustain and hide the prophets that Izevel wanted to kill.

Accomplishment..................Ovadyah saved 100 prophets and hid them in 2 caves.

Reward............................Because of his good deed, Ovadyah was rewarded to become prophet.

Book............................. The Book of Ovadyah was the shortest in the Tanach with only 21 verses.

Samuel
Patience

Who?................................	Son of Elkanah and Hannah. Born 2831 and died 2883. Was nazir who was born circumcised. Succeeded Eili, the High Priest, at 39. Was called *Roeh, Man of G-d*. One of the 8 princes in Jewish history.
Tribe.................................	Levi
Personality........................	Samuel was always self suficient. Traveled from place to place to teach and judge the people.
Challenge...........................	The People asked him for a king. Later, they insisted that they really need a king.
Accomplishments.................	Annointed Shaul, the first king of Israel. Later, annointed the second king, David. Wrote the books of Samuel and Judges.

King Shlomo
Understanding Heart

Who?.................................Son of David
Born 2912 and died 2964
Reigned for 4 years
Was prophet and received prophecy

Prayer............................. Prayed Hashem for only one thing.
Asked Hashem for and understanding heart.

Brought 1000 offerings to Hashem

Accomplishments.................Built the House of Hashem
Finished the Temple in 7 1/2 years
(2935). Famous for his wisdom:
Wrote Mishlei, Kohelet and Shir
Hashirim

Yechezkel Ben Buzi
Sensitivity

Who?................................Son of Yirmiyahu
Called by Hashem Ben-Adam
because Yechezkel had high
expectations about Him.
Last of major prophets who
prophesied to the Jews in the
Exile of Babel

Teachings..........................Heart of stone is a heart
that is insensitive.
Refering to the yetzer ha
as a stone. We need to develop a
heart of flesh that allows
us to perform mitzvoth out
of love to Hashem.
We can rejuvenate ourselves.

Personality........................Was careful with his thoughts
Was careful with the food he ate

Challenges........................he Sages wanted to concealed his
book, Yechezkel, which consists of 48
chapters. Chananyah Ben Hizkiyah
saved this book from being
concealed.

Yehoshua Bin Nun
READINESS

Birth……………………2406–2516

Tribe………………….Ephraim

Accomplishments………..Moshe's successor

Led Jewish Nation for 28 years

Moshe Rabeinu's greatest disciple

Wrote Book of Yehoshua

Personality……………… Ready to go to serve his master

Personal Counselor

Was called Youth (Na'ar) because didn't move from Moshe's tent.

Yirmiyahu Ben Chizkiyahu
Look Forward

Who?.............................Son Of Chizkiyahu
                                 Born on the 9th of Av
                                 His name means "Hashem's judgement should be elevated"
                                 He wrote his own book "Yirmiyahu", "Melachim" (Kings) and "Eicha" (Lamentations)

Time................................ When the Temple of Jerusalem was destroyed

Main Teacher......................Tzefanyah
Main Disciple......................Baruch Ben Neryah

Teachings..........................To have hope in the redemption. Asked the people to study the Torah. Inspired people to do Teshuvah (correct their ways). Not to be held by the past.
His main Saying...................."If you return, Yisrael, you will come back to Hashem"

Yonah Ben Amitai
Teshuvah

Who?.............................Son of Amitai
Child whom Eliyahu revived
Became a prophet when he arrived at Jerusalem on Simchat Bet Hashoeva. The meaning of his name in Hebrew is dove, a kosher bird, loyal to its owner. Wealthy Went to Gan Eden without dying.

Main Teacher......................Eliyahu

Teachings.........................Sometimes we are reluctant about a task that could the one with the greatest life purpose. Taught lessons on how to achieve our purpose in life.

Teshuvah..........................We read the book of Yonah on Mincha of Yom Kippur because it consists of lessons to rectify ourselves.

Zecharyah Ben Ido Meshulam

Who?......................Son of Berachyah
Granson of Ido
Zecharyah is also called Meshulam.
Meshulam means completeness.
One of the last 3 prophets

Personality...........................Zecharyah was perfect and complete in his ways.
Began his prophecy as a youth.

Teachings...........................We have to distant ourselves from lies.
Speak the truth to each other.

Accomplishment....................Was part of the Sages Great Assembly.

Yerushalaim.........................He called the City of Yerushalaim, the City of Truth.

Book....................................The Book Zecharyah is the 11th. section of Trei Asar. It consists of 14 chapters.

Amos
Focus on the Present

Who?..............................3rd. of the 12 prophets of Trei Asar

He was one of the 8 distinguished leaders in history.
Wealthy as most of the prophets
He is one of the 8 prophets who prophesied even after the destruction of the Temple.

Main Disciple......................Yeshaya
Main Teacher.....................Hoshea

Teachings.........................Torah = Seek Me (Hashem) and live.
  Focus on the Present.
  Teaches people to prepare for prayer.

Chavakuk
Cling to the Torah

Who?..............................Was the child who was born to the Shunamite woman. Elisha said to the Shunamite woman that she will "embrace" a child. His name comes from the Hebrew "lachbok" which means to "embrace" or to cling.

One of the main prophets who prophesied after the destruction of the Temple of Jerusalem.

Main Teacher......................Nachum

Main Disciple.....................Tzefanyah

Teachings.........................Torah means when a righteous person lives by his faith.

Gematria..........................Chabakuk in Hebrew add up to 216, as well as Aryeh (lion).

King David
Tehillim

Who?.................................Son of Yishai
Born 2854 and died 2924.
Was 30 when became king.
Reigned for 40 years:
7 years in Yehuda, 6 months in Hevron
33 years in Yerushalaim.
Shepherd of Hashem.
Greatest king.
His name appears in Tanach more than any other in History. One of 13 men born circumcised.

Prayer............................... Received prophetic messages from prophets Samuel, Gad and Natan. Aspired to sit in the House of Hashem always.

Accomplishments.................Composed the Book of Tehillim (Psalms written by 10 elders).

Legacy............................. Despise no person and belittle nothing. Cry out to Hashem for Success. Learn Torah. Melave Malka, the Meal of David, on Saturday night after Havdalah.

Glossary

Beresheet: First book of the Torah, Five Books of Moses

Galut: Any place outside of the land of Israel.

Haftarah: Portion taken from the Prophets read after the reading of the Torah on Shabbat.

Halacha: The complete body of rules and practicas the Jews are bound to practice.

Hashem: The name of G-d the is not pronounced.

Hashgachat Peratit: Everything that happens is supervised by G-d

Kohen: Jewish priest who blesses the Jewish community.

Kohen Gadol: He is the High Priest. The first one was Aaron, Moses' brother.

Levush: a ten-volume codification of Jewish law that particularly stressed the customs of the Jews of Eastern Europe and written by Rabbi Mordechai Jaffe, 1530.

Glossary

Mashiach: A man who will be chosen by G-d to put an end to all evil in the world.

Midrash: It is a form of Rabbinic Literature.

Mitzvoth: Any of the 613 commandments and good deeds.

Nazir: A person who dedicares himself to G-d, abstain from wine and cutting his hair.

References

The Midrash Says On Weekly Haftaros, By Rabbi Moshe Weissman, Brooklyn, NY, 1993

One Minute Messages, Eternal Lessons from Our Prophets, By Moshe Goldberger, A Targum Press Book, 2008

The Author

Ms. Malca was born in Panama City, Panama from a warm and caring family. She speaks Spanish, English and Hebrew and enjoys communicating in these three languages. Ms. Malca taught school children how to use the computer and later, she became a professional tutor. Her first book, For Your Own Good, was about the portions of the Torah. Then, These Are The Blessings of the Torah was published a year after n 2004.

She also writes children's story books. Among them are The Drops of Water and The Pieces of Bread. Ms. Malca teaches about the Weekly Torah Portion by phone and tutors students in person and online.

© Copyright 2018
By Malca Bassan
Miami, Florida

The rights of the copyright holder will be strictly enforced.

Rimonim Books

Printed in the U.S.A. by KDP.COM
Typesetting by Malca Bassan

mbassan27@gmail.com

www.ingramcontent.com/pod-product-compliance
Lightning Source LLC
Chambersburg PA
CBHW041513220426
43668CB00002B/10